The Un-Haggadah

HOW TO KEEP THE CONVERSATION
AND WINE FLOWING AT YOUR SEDER

Rabbi Mitchell Wohlberg

Publication of this book was made
possible through the generosity of:

RACHEL AND AHARON DAHAN

AND

ROZ AND MARVIN H. WEINER

Make for yourself a Rabbi and acquire for yourself a friend.
-Ethics of the Fathers

Every Rabbi should be blessed with friends like these.

This book is dedicated to my family for making the Seder the highlight of the year and my home the highlight of my life.

TABLE OF CONTENTS

INTRODUCTION

It has been pointed out that there is a new series of four questions that are asked at the Seder.

1. When do we eat?
2. How long will this take?
3. Do we have to read the whole thing?
4. Do we have to do it again tomorrow night?

This is the sad state in many American Jewish homes, but for some there is something even sadder: the four children of the Haggadah are now five; the fifth child is the one who doesn't even come to the Seder.

The Seder should be the most significant family event in the Jewish home. It is one of the rare times of the year when the entire family comes together. But that doesn't always bring out the best in us. When Conan O'Brien asked Ellen Barkin about her Pesach Seder, she described her family's Seders as "foul mouthed, shouting matches." At one, her father threw the brisket across the table at her mother!

Often Seders fail because of a lack of preparation. So much time and effort go into preparing the food, but so little time and effort are spent on preparing what to talk about at the Seder. Despite the more than 3000 different editions of the Haggadah that are now available, families find themselves at a loss for words in trying to make the ancient story relevant.

The purpose of this book is to do just that. Although it contains the text, this book is not meant to be a Haggadah. This book is not a commentary on the Haggadah. This book is a series of thoughts relating to themes that are presented in the Haggadah. The subjects covered range from matzah to Mel Gibson … Kabbalah to karpas … afikoman to anti-Semitism … maror to Madonna … and all points in between. Each thought relates to the contemporary American Jew and ends with one or more questions to help family discussion flow … along with the wine!

All of us have memories from the Seder of our parents or grandparents. It is the author's hope that this book will help make your Seder a meaningful one for your children and grandchildren, providing all the participants with memories to cherish.

Mitchell Wohlberg

KADESH
WE MAKE KIDDUSH.

In keeping with the statement found in the Book of Proverbs: "*Yayin yisamach levav enosh* – wine rejoices the heart of man," wine plays an important role in the joyous celebrations of the Jews. Every Sabbath and festival is ushered in with wine; every simcha – bris, wedding – is celebrated with wine. But at no time is wine more prevalent than during Pesach. Four times at the Seder, we pour a glass of wine and make a blessing over it. The drinking of the four cups of wine at the Seder has such great significance that whereas normally if one cannot afford to perform a mitzvah (for example, if you do not have enough money to buy a lulav and etrog on Sukkot), Jewish law exempts you, but not so when it comes to the four cups. There the *Code of Jewish Law* tells us, "Even a poor person who is subsidized by charity should rent or sell his cloak or hire himself out for hire to purchase wine for the four cups." Yes, wine is essential to the Pesach experience.

In this spirit, in recent years in the weeks leading up to Pesach *The Wall Street Journal* has featured an article listing "The Dow Jones Kosher Wine Index." There are now thousands of different kinds of kosher wines, including Roija from Spain, Macon from France, Malbec from Chile and Bulsblood from Hungary. And *The Wall Street Journal*'s professional wine experts give their recommendations of what wine you should serve at the Seder.

Do we understand how remarkable this is? Do we understand what a change this represents? In the 1600's Rabbi David Halevi, better known as the "Taz," wrote an important commentary on the *Code of Jewish Law*. In his commentary the Taz made a remarkable ruling. He explained that whereas traditionally it is preferable to use red wine at the Seder, "in our times we refrain from using red wine for the four cups because of the libelous slanders which we have endured."

Those words of the Taz go to the heart of centuries of turmoil Jews experienced because of the Pesach wine. Until rather recently the wine that Jews used, especially on Pesach, was the source of countless tragedies and the murder of thousands of Jews who were accused of having murdered Christian children, so as to use their blood to make the wine for the Pesach Seder. This blood libel swept across all of Christian Europe. It started in Norwich, England in 1144. Eleven years later, 19 Jews were hanged in Lincoln, England. A few years later the blood libel came to France. In 1648 it was Poland's turn. In each case, the story was usually the same: a child was found dead and the Jews were accused of murdering him and using his blood for ritual purposes. This, despite the fact that even animal blood is forbidden for any ritual purpose according to Jewish law.

The 20th century started with the infamous Mendel Beiliss case in Russia, in which a Jew was accused of the blood libel. And now comes the 21st century in America and we have the "Dow Jones Kosher Wine Index!" Only in America! America, in some ways, has become the "Goldener Medinah" – the golden land for the Jews.

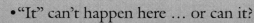

?
- "It" can't happen here … or can it?
- Why is it that only the Jews have an "it" to worry about?
- Will anti-Semitism ever really go away?
- Do you know an anti-Semite?

4

קַדֵּשׁ

(לְשַׁבָּת: וַיְהִי עֶרֶב וַיְהִי בֹקֶר יוֹם הַשִּׁשִּׁי: וַיְכֻלּוּ הַשָּׁמַיִם וְהָאָרֶץ
וְכָל-צְבָאָם: וַיְכַל אֱלֹהִים בַּיּוֹם הַשְּׁבִיעִי, מְלַאכְתּוֹ אֲשֶׁר עָשָׂה, וַיִּשְׁבּוֹת
בַּיּוֹם הַשְּׁבִיעִי, מִכָּל-מְלַאכְתּוֹ אֲשֶׁר עָשָׂה: וַיְבָרֶךְ אֱלֹהִים אֶת-יוֹם
הַשְּׁבִיעִי, וַיְקַדֵּשׁ אֹתוֹ, כִּי בוֹ שָׁבַת מִכָּל-מְלַאכְתּוֹ, אֲשֶׁר-בָּרָא
אֱלֹהִים לַעֲשׂוֹת:)

סַבְרִי מָרָנָן וְרַבָּנָן וְרַבּוֹתַי:
בָּרוּךְ אַתָּה יהוה, אֱלֹהֵינוּ מֶלֶךְ הָעוֹלָם, בּוֹרֵא פְּרִי הַגָּפֶן:
בָּרוּךְ אַתָּה יהוה, אֱלֹהֵינוּ מֶלֶךְ הָעוֹלָם, אֲשֶׁר בָּחַר בָּנוּ מִכָּל-עָם, וְרוֹמְמָנוּ
מִכָּל-לָשׁוֹן, וְקִדְּשָׁנוּ בְּמִצְוֹתָיו. וַתִּתֶּן-לָנוּ יהוה אֱלֹהֵינוּ בְּאַהֲבָה
(לְשַׁבָּת: שַׁבָּתוֹת לִמְנוּחָה וּ) מוֹעֲדִים לְשִׂמְחָה, חַגִּים וּזְמַנִּים לְשָׂשׂוֹן,
אֶת-יוֹם (לְשַׁבָּת: הַשַּׁבָּת הַזֶּה וְאֶת-יוֹם) חַג הַמַּצּוֹת הַזֶּה. זְמַן חֵרוּתֵינוּ,
(לְשַׁבָּת: בְּאַהֲבָה,) מִקְרָא קֹדֶשׁ, זֵכֶר לִיצִיאַת מִצְרָיִם. כִּי בָנוּ בָחַרְתָּ

Kadesh ~Hebrew (only) ~~deft text~~.

*The kiddush should not be recited before nightfall. Each person's cup should be filled by
someone else and should hold at least 87-112 grams, or 2.5-3.3 fl. oz of wine. The wine
should be drunk without delay, reclining on the left side. It is preferable to use red wine. It
is also preferable to drink the entire cup, but at the very least, most of the wine should be
drunk.*

On Friday night add:

(There was evening and there was morning, on the sixth day. The heavens
and the earth and all their hosts were completed. And God completed,
on the seventh day, His work, which He had made, and He ceased on the
seventh day, from all His work in which He had been engaged. And God
blessed the seventh day and sanctified it; because on it He ceased from all
His work which in creation God had made.)

God, You are the source of blessing, our God, King of the universe, Who
creates the fruit of the vine.

God, You are the source of blessing, our God, King of the universe, Who
has chosen and exalted us above all nations and has sanctified us with His
commandments. And He, Lord our God, has lovingly bestowed upon us (on
Shabbat: Sabbaths for rest and), appointed times for happiness, holidays
and seasons for joy, (on Shabbat: this Sabbath day, and) this Feast of Matzot,

5

וְאוֹתָנוּ קִדַּשְׁתָּ מִכָּל-הָעַמִּים. (לשבת: וְשַׁבָּת) וּמוֹעֲדֵי קָדְשֶׁךָ
(לשבת: בְּאַהֲבָה וּבְרָצוֹן) בְּשִׂמְחָה וּבְשָׂשׂוֹן הִנְחַלְתָּנוּ:
בָּרוּךְ אַתָּה יהוה, מְקַדֵּשׁ (לשבת: הַשַּׁבָּת וְ) יִשְׂרָאֵל וְהַזְּמַנִּים:

On Saturday night add the paragraphs in parentheses:

(בָּרוּךְ אַתָּה יהוה, אֱלֹהֵינוּ מֶלֶךְ הָעוֹלָם, בּוֹרֵא מְאוֹרֵי הָאֵשׁ:

בָּרוּךְ אַתָּה יהוה, אֱלֹהֵינוּ מֶלֶךְ הָעוֹלָם, הַמַּבְדִּיל בֵּין קֹדֶשׁ לְחֹל, בֵּין
הַבְדָּלָתָ. אוֹר לְחֹשֶׁךְ, בֵּין יִשְׂרָאֵל לָעַמִּים, בֵּין יוֹם הַשְּׁבִיעִי לְשֵׁשֶׁת יְמֵי
הַמַּעֲשֶׂה. בֵּין קְדֻשַּׁת שַׁבָּת לִקְדֻשַּׁת יוֹם טוֹב וְאֶת-יוֹם הַשְּׁבִיעִי
מִשֵּׁשֶׁת יְמֵי הַמַּעֲשֶׂה קִדַּשְׁתָּ. הִבְדַּלְתָּ וְקִדַּשְׁתָּ אֶת-עַמְּךָ יִשְׂרָאֵל
בִּקְדֻשָּׁתֶךָ. בָּרוּךְ אַתָּה יהוה, הַמַּבְדִּיל בֵּין קֹדֶשׁ לְקֹדֶשׁ:)

בָּרוּךְ אַתָּה יהוה, אֱלֹהֵינוּ מֶלֶךְ הָעוֹלָם, שֶׁהֶחֱיָנוּ וְקִיְּמָנוּ וְהִגִּיעָנוּ לַזְּמַן הַזֶּה:

---

our season of freedom, a holy convocation recalling the Exodus from Egypt. You did choose us and sanctify us above all peoples. In Your gracious love, You granted us Your (on Shabbat: holy Sabbath, and) appointed times for happiness and joy. God, You are the source of blessing, Who sanctifies (on Shabbat: the Sabbath), Israel, and the appointed times.

On Saturday night add the paragraphs in parentheses:

(God, You are the source of blessing, our God, King of the universe, Who creates the light of the fire.

God, You are the source of blessing, our God, King of the universe, Who has distinguished between the sacred and the secular, between light and darkness, between Israel and the nations, between the seventh day and the six working days. You have distinguished between the holiness of the Sabbath and the holiness of the Festival, and have sanctified the seventh day above the six working days. You have distinguished and sanctified Your people Israel with Your holiness. God, You are the source of blessing, Who distinguishes between the degrees of holiness.)

God, You are the source of blessing, our God, King of the universe, Who has granted us life and sustenance and permitted us to reach this time.

Washing Hands (without a blessing)

The head of the household (according to many opinions, all participants in the Seder) washes his hands by pouring water from a cup twice over his right hand and twice over his left hand. No blessing is recited at this time.

Karpas
Dip a Vegetable in Salt Water

The dipping of a vegetable into salt water at the beginning of the Seder is one of the stranger Passover rituals. Every aspect of it is questioned.

- Why do we wash our hands before eating the karpas? And why do we wash without a blessing?
- Do we first say the blessing over the vegetable and then dip, or first dip and then say the blessing?
- What do we dip the vegetable into? While it is generally understood that we dip it into salt water, Maimonides says that it should be dipped into charoset.
- What do we dip? Most authorities say any green vegetable. And yet, many Jews use a potato.

But perhaps the most important question is: why are we doing this? What is this ritual's real meaning? The fact is, no one knows for sure. According to the Talmud the only reason for this ritual is to evoke questions from the children present at the Seder. Another explanation is that "karpas" is the Greek word for "grass" or "vegetation," and Pesach, the spring festival, is the time when the greenery begins to sprout. Yet another thought is to rearrange the letters in the word "karpas" to be read backward; the Hebrew letter *samech*, having the numerical value of 60, represents the 600,000 male Jews who left Egypt. The rest of the word, now reading "*perach*," meaning "to break," reminds us of the backbreaking work the Jews experienced in the land of Egypt.

A novel approach is found in the Haggadah of the 19ᵗʰ century scholar of Baghdad, the Ben Ish Chai, who sees the dipping of karpas in salt water as a reminder of how Joseph's brothers immersed his coat in the goat's blood. Ben Ish Chai takes note of the fact that when the Torah speaks of the "*kutonet passim*", Joseph's coat of many colors, the great

Biblical commentator, Rashi, surprisingly comments, *"K'mo karpas* – like fine linen." Karpas – "fine linen."

In linking the karpas to the incident of Joseph and his brothers we find a meaningful reason why this ritual takes place at the beginning of the Pesach Seder. Before we speak of our enslavement in Egypt, it is necessary first to remind ourselves of what led to this enslavement. It all started when Joseph's brothers sold him into slavery in Egypt. It started when brothers turned against brothers.

One of the battle cries of the American Jewish community has long been, "We are one!" But is that really true? In his award winning book, Jew vs. Jew, Samuel Freedman points out how divided we are as a people. From Great Neck, New York to the Western Wall in Jerusalem, we find Jews fighting against their fellow Jews. "Secularist against believer, denomination against denomination, gender against gender, liberal against conservative, traditionalist against modernist – even within each branch," says Freedman. In some ways it boils down to two kinds of Jews. One is committed to klal Yisrael as defined by our people's modern "Mitzvah Man," Danny Siegel.

> Klal Yisrael means all Jews – everyone: Jewish prisoners,
> IQ-deficient Jews, Jews with an extra chromosome who
> languish in non-Jewish homes because no Jews will take
> them in, battered Jews, Jews who are old-time Yiddish
> speaking Socialists, alcoholic Jews and Jewish drug abusers,
> rich and poor Jews and middle income Jews, Orthodox
> Jews, fancy-schmancy Jews, downtrodden and lonely
> Jews, the burned Jews and the scarred Jews (by accident
> or by defense of the Homeland), the deformed Jews and
> ugly Jews as well as the gorgeous ones. Jews with AIDS
> and nowhere to go in some Jewish communities, elderly
> Jews (Moses told Pharaoh that they would leave Egypt
> with the old and young alike), Reform Jews, hungry
> Jews and the ones who can't afford a decent Passover
> or Purim, or any Passover or Purim at all, or have no
> family in the whole world to eat Shabbos dinner with,

Reconstructionist Jews, homeless Jews, unemployed Jews, displaced Jews, suicidal Jews, imglicklich Jews, i.e., Jews who have never had any luck in life, sad Jews, caring and callous Jews, Jews who are hot shots and Jews who are shleppers, crooked and honest Jews, Soviet Jews who would be free and involved and Soviet Jews who would be free and uninvolved, Jews living in terror and Jews unaware of the blessings of life, liberty and the pursuit of happiness or unable to attain those blessings, Jews who used to be non-Jews, insightful and dull and boring Jews, scholarly and ignorant Jews, wise and foolish Jews, active and committed and assimilated Jews, Jews who are hypocrites and Jews who are sincere, insensitive Jews and those who can't sleep at night for the suffering of Klal Yisrael. And that is just some small portion of the Jewish people!

The second kind of Jew is found in the anecdote told by Rabbi Harold Schulweis, where one Chasid is talking to another:

The whole world is divided between "them and "us," he says. No point speaking about "them." Among "us" the world is divided between Askenazim and Sephardim. No use talking about Sephardim. Among Ashkenazim the world is divided between Hasidim and Mitnagdim. No use talking about Mitnagdim. Among the Hasidim, the world is divided between the Satmar and the Lubavitcher. No use talking about the Satmar. Among the Lubavitcher there are the intellectual and the farbrengen types. No use to talk about the latter. Among the intellectuals there are you and me. And you know how little you know!

Which kind of Jew are you?

One of the classic works of Jewish thought is the *Tanya* – the great work of the first Lubavitcher Rebbe. In the 32nd chapter of this work, the Rebbe sets out the idea that all Jews are mystically united; their bodies

9

are separate but their souls are one. They share, as it were, a single collective spiritual substance.

• Do you believe this to be true?
• Do you love all Jews?
• Are some Jews not loveable? Why?
• Do you look at a Jew differently if he/she is Orthodox? Secular?

כַּרְפַּס

Everyone should take a vegetable other than marror and dip it into salt water. A piece smaller in volume than half an egg (1.1-1.25 oz.) should be used. The following blessing is recited before eating the vegetable, with the intention that it also applies to the marror, which will be eaten later. It is recommended that one not recline while eating it. It is preferable that those who did not wash their hands at urchatz do not touch the vegetable with their hands, but use a utensil.

בָּרוּךְ אַתָּה יהוה, אֱלֹהֵינוּ מֶלֶךְ הָעוֹלָם, בּוֹרֵא פְּרִי הָאֲדָמָה:

יַחַץ

The head of the household breaks the middle matzah in two. He puts the smaller part back between the two whole matzot and wraps up the larger portion for later use as the afikoman. It is preferable that enough matzah for all participants be set aside with the afikoman. The remaining matzah should be the equivalent of the volume of half an egg, (1.1- 1.25 oz.).

Dipping Vegetable in Salt Water

Everyone should take a vegetable other than marror and dip it into salt water. A piece smaller in volume than half an egg (1.1-1.25 oz.) should be used. The following blessing is recited before eating the vegetable, with the intention that it also applies to the marror, which will be eaten later. It is recommended that one not recline while eating it. It is preferable that those who did not wash their hands at urchatz do not touch the vegetable with their hands, but use a utensil.

God, You are the source of blessing, our God, King of the universe, Who creates the fruit of the earth.

Breaking of the Middle Matzah

The head of the household breaks the middle matzah in two. He puts the smaller part back between the two whole matzot and wraps up the larger portion for later use as the afikoman. It is preferable that enough matzah for all participants be set aside with the afikoman. The remaining matzah should be the equivalent of the volume of half an egg, (1.1- 1.25 oz.).

Maggid
Telling The Story

The Seder begins with the telling of the story of our Egyptian experience by first inviting others to our Pesach Seder, proclaiming that "all who are hungry come and eat, whoever is needy come and celebrate Pesach."

Celebrating the Pesach Seder as we do nowadays – in hotels, on the French Riviera, in Antigua, Venice, Barcelona and Disney World – do we really mean it when we say, "Let all who are hungry come and eat, whoever is needy come and celebrate Pesach"?

As Americans we are living in a time of political and social revolution. For a long time many felt that in regard to the poor and needy, money would make all the difference in the world. They were wrong. So there's now a new ideology: that money makes no difference; equally wrong! The new political correctness exalts heartlessness and says, "Let the poor pull themselves up by their bootstraps as we did," even though many of those "we's" were able to make it in America only because of government subsidies and programs.

There is a changing mood in our country that enables us to walk over homeless people and talk about orphanages without blinking an eye, that has poor people compared to wolves and alligators on the floor of Congress. We used to be allowed to feel good about the ethical underpinning that commanded us to help those less fortunately endowed than ourselves. But now many in our government and society have adopted the notion that a helping hand is nothing more than an insidious handout. Helping the sick, the poor, and the old, we are told, saps human will and challenge. None of the government programs helping them was what they really needed.

The reality is that Jews, like so many others, are no longer as concerned with social justice and human rights as they used to be. Among Jews today very little is heard about the poor, the underprivileged, the plight of the minorities.

Are Jews still liberals? Are they becoming conservatives? Much is being written about this these days, but the reality is Jews should reject the false promises of both the left and the right. The poor, the sick and the needy are confronted by difficulties that do not have ideological names. The Torah is above political partisanship when it looks at the experience of the Jews in Egypt. Lessons can be found there that both liberals and conservatives, Republicans and Democrats, could and should agree on. According to the late, great Rabbi Joseph B. Soloveitchik, the Jews' enslavement in Egypt "taught the Jew ethical sensitivity, what it truly means to be a Jew. It sought to transform the Jew into a rachaman, one possessing a heightened form of ethical sensitivity and responsiveness." Whenever the Torah wishes to impress upon us the mitzvah of having compassion and sympathy for the oppressed in society, it reminds us of our similar helplessness and lowly status during our bondage in Egypt. And you know how many times the Torah does this? 36 times -- 36 times in the Torah we are commanded to treat the less fortunate kindly because: *"Ki gerim hayitem b'eretz mitzrayim* -- You were strangers in the land of Egypt." And therefore: *"V'atem yedatem et nefesh ha'ger"* -- Having experienced estrangement, oppression, and discrimination, you are expected, more so than one who hasn't, to empathize and sympathize with the needy."

Molly Picon, speaking about life on the Lower East Side of New York said, "There were six of us in that one bedroom apartment. Even so, company was always coming to stay with us for weeks at a time. When someone would call attention to the crowded apartment, my mother would answer: 'Where there is room in the heart, there is always room in the house.'"

- Are Jews still at the forefront in the battles for civil rights, workers' rights and gender equality?
- Have Jews become more conservative?
- Does being Jewish and being liberal go hand-in-hand?

מַגִּיד

The matzot are lifted, and the following is recited. The Haggadah is to be recited with reverence and thus one should not recline.

הָא לַחְמָא עַנְיָא דִי אֲכָלוּ אַבְהָתָנָא בְּאַרְעָא דְמִצְרָיִם. כָּל דִּכְפִין יֵיתֵי
וְיֵכוּל, כָּל דִּצְרִיךְ יֵיתֵי וְיִפְסַח. הָשַׁתָּא הָכָא, לְשָׁנָה הַבָּאָה בְּאַרְעָא
דְיִשְׂרָאֵל. הָשַׁתָּא עַבְדֵי, לְשָׁנָה הַבָּאָה בְּנֵי חוֹרִין:

The Seder Plate is removed from the room, and the second of the four cups of wine is poured.

Recitation of the Haggadah

The matzot are lifted, and the following is recited. The Haggadah is to be recited with reverence and thus one should not recline.

This is the bread of affliction which our fathers ate in the land of Egypt. Let all who are hungry come and eat. Let all who are needy come and celebrate the Passover. At present we are here; next year may we be in the land of Israel. At present we are slaves; next year may we be free.

The Seder Plate is removed from the room, and the second of the four cups of wine is poured.

14

MAH NISHTANAH
WHY IS THIS NIGHT ...?

The asking of the four questions by children has become the most popular moment at the Seder. Question: Where did this idea of the four questions come from? Answer: It is found in a Mishnah in the Tractate *Pesachim* where we are told: "They poured the second cup of wine and here the child asks his father. But if the child lacks the knowledge the father teaches him: *'Ma nishtana halayla hazeh.'*" It matters not who asks the question as long as questions are asked. In fact, the Talmud tells us a story of little Abaye who was about to begin his Pesach Seder when the servants removed the Seder plate. Shocked by the servants' actions, little Abaye asked his teacher Rabbah: "Why did they take away the plate? We haven't eaten yet." To this, his teacher responded: "By your question, you have exempted us from reciting the Ma Nishtana."

The bottom line is, the Mishnah's concern is not who asks the question and not what is the question. The Mishnah's concern is that a question be asked. Because without a question the story can't be told.

Jews have become identified with asking questions. The old joke -- You ask a Jew, "How come you Jews ask so many questions?" He answers – "Why not?" Questioning is important for several reasons. It is certainly appropriate for a Seder night because questioning is a sign of freedom. If we are permitted to attempt to make sense out of our surroundings... if we are permitted to question, challenge, investigate, probe...if we are permitted to ask, inquire, and search...then we know we are free. But it is more than this. Tom Peters once said, "In the brain-based economy, victory goes to the perpetually curious." Judaism is a brain-based economy. We aren't the people of the book for nothing. Some of the most important pieces of Jewish literature are the Responsa, questions and answers on issues of Jewish law and doctrine. Only by asking the questions do we learn. The Nobel physicist, Isaac Rabi, was asked to what he attributes his success in the field of science. He responded,

"Whenever I returned home from school as a child my mother never asked me, 'Ike, what did you learn today?' She always asked, 'Ike, did you ask a good question?'"

But there is one more reason why asking questions is important. It reminds us that we are human, that only God knows all the answers. The rest of us are frail, fallible human beings, who often make mistakes, even about things we are certain we know. Just ask George Tenet, the former head of the CIA. He might not have become the "former" head if he hadn't told President Bush that it was a "slam dunk" that Iraq had weapons of mass destruction. One of the problems in America's political life today is that everyone has become so sure of himself. Republicans and Democrats, liberals and conservatives have always disagreed, but never before have the divisions been so vitriolic, leaving no possibility that there just might be some small measure of truth in the other side's position. Everyone is so sure that he is right!

Rashi wasn't! It's almost impossible to study the Bible or the Talmud without using Rashi's commentary. And yet, in his commentary, more than 100 times you'll find Rashi writing, "I don't know what this means." Now, Rashi didn't have to write that! He didn't have to write anything! We would never know. But then, we never would have known how great Rashi was. His greatness is reflected not only in what he knew, but in the fact that he was willing to admit what he didn't know.

You know who was very lucky? Rashi's wife and children. One of the most negative comments you can make about a person is to say, "He's a Mr. Know-it-all." Many of us grew up with a person like that in our lives. Many of us can testify from our personal lives about having had a parent or teacher who was dogmatic, intransigent, unwilling to allow for any discussion or give and take. In style and in substance they were so smug, so certain, so authoritarian. There is a thin line separating love, caring and concern, from dominance, subjugation, and control. Do you know anyone like that? Someone who thinks he's always right? Do you live with someone like that? Many husband-wife relationships and parent-child relationships suffer from this syndrome. There can be no communication over any disagreements. I suspect it wasn't like this in Rashi's household. He was "man" enough to admit that he didn't know it all! Only God is infallible. We, as finite, frail, limited, mortal human beings, must always recognize that little in life is certain or immutable. We dare not be a Mr. Know-it-all.

- Is there a "know-it-all" at your Seder?
- Are you married to a "know-it-all?"
- Are you one?
- Any questions?

מַה נִּשְׁתַּנָּה הַלַּיְלָה הַזֶּה מִכָּל-הַלֵּילוֹת?

שֶׁבְּכָל-הַלֵּילוֹת אָנוּ אוֹכְלִין חָמֵץ וּמַצָּה. הַלַּיְלָה הַזֶּה כֻּלּוֹ מַצָּה:

שֶׁבְּכָל-הַלֵּילוֹת אָנוּ אוֹכְלִין שְׁאָר יְרָקוֹת. הַלַּיְלָה הַזֶּה מָרוֹר:

אֶחָת. הַלַּיְלָה הַזֶּה שְׁתֵּי פְעָמִים:

שֶׁבְּכָל-הַלֵּילוֹת אֵין אָנוּ מַטְבִּילִין אֲפִילוּ פַּעַם אֶחָת. הַלַּיְלָה הַזֶּה
שְׁתֵּי פְעָמִים:

שֶׁבְּכָל-הַלֵּילוֹת אָנוּ אוֹכְלִין בֵּין יוֹשְׁבִין וּבֵין מְסֻבִּין. הַלַּיְלָה הַזֶּה
כֻּלָּנוּ מְסֻבִּין:

Why is this night different from all other nights?

1. On all other nights we eat chametz and matzah. Tonight, we eat only matzah.

2. On all other nights we eat any kind of vegetable. Tonight, we eat the bitter herbs.

3. On all other nights we do not dip even once. Tonight, we dip twice.

4. On all other nights we eat sitting or reclining. Tonight, we all recline.

AVADIM HAYEINU
WE WERE SLAVES.

"We were slaves unto Pharaoh in Egypt." This is what Pesach is all about! This is the foundation of our national existence. This forms the basis for the first of the Ten Commandments, "I am the Lord thy God who took you out of the land of Egypt, the house of bondage."

Did you ever wonder why it had to say both "the land of Egypt" and "the house of bondage?" Aren't they the same? Did you ever wonder why this prayer continues with the words, "Had not the Holy One, praised be He, brought our ancestors out of Egypt, then we and our children and our children's children would still be enslaved to Pharaoh in Egypt?" Really? Still? After all these years? And what of the earlier proclamation we made, "*Hashatah avdei* – now we are slaves." Really? Do you feel like a slave in America?

Perhaps the message of Passover is that human slavery is created not only by chains and whips, but frequently we enslave ourselves. Our ancestors were slaves to Pharaoh in Egypt, but all too many of us are slaves to money and our jobs.

Thomas Friedman, Pulitzer Prize winning columnist for *The New York Times*, claims that the following news item, to him, is most descriptive of our current condition. The story, coming from Israel, said that a traffic policeman pulled over a driver in Netanya and gave the man a ticket for driving with a cell phone in each hand. He was steering the car with his elbows and the car was weaving from side to side.

Between our cell phones, faxes, e-mails and Blackberries, we never really leave the office. We never really relax; we're always wired, even when we're wireless. Too many make the mistake of thinking their career is their life. And so, they never give themselves completely to their children and spouses because there is always a business call waiting, always another deal to make, always another client to get back to. And it's 24/7.

There's an ad for a small light for your laptop computer so that "when you take your computer to bed you will not disturb your spouse." Previous generations taught you that one of the reasons you got married was so that you could get into bed and disturb your spouse! But now … no time for spouse, for children, for relaxation, for fun. Not in the world of 24/7.

Pesach comes to liberate us from our enslavement to the drives within us, as well as from the taskmasters outside of us.

• Are you still enslaved?
• Have you ever considered using Shabbat as a time to un-plug and unwind?
• Do you have a "day of rest?"
• Would you like to have one?
• What's stopping you?

עֲבָדִים הָיִינוּ לְפַרְעֹה בְּמִצְרָיִם. וַיּוֹצִיאֵנוּ יְהֹוָה אֱלֹהֵינוּ מִשָּׁם, בְּיָד חֲזָקָה וּבִזְרוֹעַ נְטוּיָה, וְאִלּוּ לֹא הוֹצִיא הַקָּדוֹשׁ בָּרוּךְ הוּא אֶת־אֲבוֹתֵינוּ מִמִּצְרַיִם, הֲרֵי אָנוּ וּבָנֵינוּ וּבְנֵי בָנֵינוּ, מְשֻׁעְבָּדִים הָיִינוּ לְפַרְעֹה בְּמִצְרָיִם. וַאֲפִילוּ כֻּלָּנוּ חֲכָמִים, כֻּלָּנוּ נְבוֹנִים, כֻּלָּנוּ זְקֵנִים, כֻּלָּנוּ יוֹדְעִים אֶת־הַתּוֹרָה, מִצְוָה עָלֵינוּ לְסַפֵּר בִּיצִיאַת מִצְרָיִם. וְכָל־הַמַּרְבֶּה לְסַפֵּר בִּיצִיאַת מִצְרַיִם, הֲרֵי זֶה מְשֻׁבָּח.

We were slaves to Pharaoh in Egypt, but the Lord our God took us out of there with a mighty hand and an outstretched arm. Had not the Holy One, blessed be He, taken our fathers out of Egypt, then we, our children and grandchildren, would still be enslaved to Pharaoh in Egypt. And even if we all were wise, all were perceptive, all were experienced, and all versed in Torah, it would still be our duty to tell about the Exodus from Egypt. And whomever talks more about the Exodus from Egypt, praiseworthy is such a person.

Maaseh B'rebbe Eliezer
It Once Happened That
Rabbi Eliezer...

And

Omar Rebbe Elazar Ben Azaryeh
Rabbi Elazar Son Of Azaryah Said...

These two paragraphs describe the depth of the discussion and analysis that the rabbis of old gave to our Egyptian experience. One group of rabbis is described as staying up the entire night discussing the exodus from Egypt. The next paragraph describes the importance of remembering the exodus from Egypt not only every day but every night as well (as we do in the third paragraph of the Shema).

These discussions of our rabbis are put into doubt by the statements of some modern rabbis who question whether the exodus from Egypt ever took place. Their doubts are based on pronouncements that archaeologists have found no evidence of the Israelites in the Sinai desert. One rabbi was quoted as saying, "I long ago got to the point where we were merely an amalgam of Canaanite influence, Phoenician influence and Egyptian influences."

But if that is all we are, what makes our claim to the land of Israel stronger than that of the Arabs? If the exodus never happened, give one good reason to give up bagels for a whole week!

The danger of this mindset is reflected in an article Jonathan Rosenblum wrote in *The Jerusalem Post* relating the following story:

> Salah Tamari, a former Palestinian terrorist, told Israeli journalist Aharon Barnea of the complete transformation he underwent in a Israeli prison. While in prison he completely despaired of any hope that the Palestinians

would one day realize any of their territorial dreams and was ready to renounce the struggle.

Then, one Pesach, he witnessed his Jewish warden eating a pita sandwich. Tamari was shocked, and asked his jailer how he could so unashamedly eat bread on Pesach. The Jew replied, "I feel no obligation to events that took place over 2000 years ago. I have no connection to that.'

That entire night Tamari could not sleep. He thought to himself, 'A nation whose members have no connection to their past and are capable of so openly transgressing their most important laws . . . that nation has cut off all its roots to the Land.'

He concluded that the Palestinians could, in fact, achieve all their goals. From that moment, he determined 'to fight for everything – not a percentage, not such crumbs as the Israelis might throw us – but for everything. Because opposing us is a nation that has no connection to its roots, which are no longer of interest to it.'

The Nile is a river in Egypt. But denial is a very serious problem among Jews today.

- Do you believe the Bible is the word of God?
- What do you believe about the history of the Jewish people?
- Do you believe the Pesach story?
- If not, what are you doing here tonight?

מַעֲשֶׂה בְּרַבִּי אֱלִיעֶזֶר, וְרַבִּי יְהוֹשֻׁעַ, וְרַבִּי אֶלְעָזָר בֶּן עֲזַרְיָה, וְרַבִּי עֲקִיבָא, וְרַבִּי טַרְפוֹן, שֶׁהָיוּ מְסֻבִּין בִּבְנֵי־בְרַק, וְהָיוּ מְסַפְּרִים בִּיצִיאַת מִצְרַיִם, כָּל־אוֹתוֹ הַלַּיְלָה, עַד שֶׁבָּאוּ תַלְמִידֵיהֶם וְאָמְרוּ לָהֶם: רַבּוֹתֵינוּ, הִגִּיעַ זְמַן קְרִיאַת שְׁמַע שֶׁל שַׁחֲרִית:

אָמַר רַבִּי אֶלְעָזָר בֶּן־עֲזַרְיָה. הֲרֵי אֲנִי כְּבֶן שִׁבְעִים שָׁנָה, וְלֹא זָכִיתִי, שֶׁתֵּאָמֵר יְצִיאַת מִצְרַיִם בַּלֵּילוֹת, עַד שֶׁדְּרָשָׁהּ בֶּן זוֹמָא.

שֶׁנֶּאֱמַר: לְמַעַן תִּזְכֹּר אֶת־יוֹם צֵאתְךָ מֵאֶרֶץ מִצְרַיִם, כֹּל יְמֵי חַיֶּיךָ. יְמֵי חַיֶּיךָ הַיָּמִים. כֹּל יְמֵי חַיֶּיךָ הַלֵּילוֹת. וַחֲכָמִים אוֹמְרִים: יְמֵי חַיֶּיךָ הָעוֹלָם הַזֶּה. כֹּל יְמֵי חַיֶּיךָ לְהָבִיא לִימוֹת הַמָּשִׁיחַ:

It happened that Rabbi Eliezer, Rabbi Yehoshua, Rabbi Elazar ben Azaryah, Rabbi Akiva and Rabbi Tarfon were reclining at the Seder table in Bnei Brak. They spent the whole night discussing the Exodus from Egypt until their students came and said to them: "Rabbis, it is time for the recitation of the morning Shema."

Rabbi Elazar ben Azaryah said: "I am like a seventy-year old man and I had not succeeded in teaching why the Exodus from Egypt should be mentioned at night, until Ben Zoma explained it.

As it is said: "In order that you may remember the day you left Egypt all the days of your life." The Torah adds the word "all" to the phrase "the days of your life" to indicate that the nights are meant as well. The sages declare that "the days of your life" means the present world and "all" includes the messianic era.

BORUCH HAMAKOM
BLESSED IS GOD

We now praise and bless God. How many times? The answer should come as no surprise – four times. Four times do we find the word *"boruch* – blessed" as we say: *"Boruch Hamakom."*

WHY 4 CUPS?

Four is the number that runs through our entire Haggadah. We drink four cups, we ask four questions, we speak of four children. Why "four?" The commonly accepted answer is that four corresponds to the four expressions of redemption made by God to Moses and the children of Israel during their Egyptian enslavement. "I will bring you out; I will deliver you; I will redeem you; I will take you unto Me." (Exodus 6:6-7) There are several other reasons given for the use of four in the Haggadah:

- Four alludes to the four cups mentioned by Joseph in his interpretation of the dream of Pharoah's chief butler. (Genesis 40:11-14)
- Four symbolizes the four generations of the children of Israel who lived in Egypt.
- Four denotes the four great empires that battled against the Jews: Babylonia, Persia, Greece and Rome.

But a famous commentator, the Maharsha, gives an important explanation of the "fours" for contemporary times. He explains the use of the number four through the Haggadah is meant to remind us of the merits of our four mothers: Sarah, Rebecca, Rachel and Leah.

In recent years it has been noted that the role of women is absent from the Haggadah. This has led to the initiation of a new ritual, "the cup of Miriam", to remember the important role this woman played for the Jews in Egypt and thereafter, and to recall the significant contributions Jewish women have made ever since.

Miriam was not the only woman to play a role in our Egyptian experience. There were several who played an important role in Moses' development and the development of the Jewish people. How many? You guessed it … four … Miriam, his sister; Ziporah, his wife; Yocheved, his mother; and Batya, Pharaoh's daughter who saved him. As Rabbi Jack Riemer points out, perhaps the Torah describes all four to make the point that there is no one officially approved, acceptable model of what it means to be a woman. Instead there are four models side by side. One is woman as embodiment of mercy, like Batya who reached out her hand to save Moses from the Nile. One is woman as molder and maker of the self-image of a child during infancy, like Yocheved who helped raise Moses in Pharaoh's palace. One is woman as "macher" who fights and leads to the extent that she can, like Miriam. And one is woman as housewife, like Ziporah who does – don't knock it and don't minimize it – the indispensable task of maintaining a home, caring for a husband and raising two children.

Yes, there are many acceptable and legitimate roles for a woman to play. And some women fill all four roles. It's their choice, and they need not apologize or brag or compare themselves with anyone who has chosen a different way of being a woman.

But whatever role a woman chooses, it is fairly safe to say that it was a woman who played a leading role in making tonight's Seder possible. As someone wrote:

Wouldn't you think that the person who plans,
The person who changes the pots and pans,
The person who suffers the elbowing crowd,
And brings home the matzah meal, bloody and bowed,
Who battles the butcher, accumulates plates
And races the clock to those Passover dates.
Who polishes silverware, commandeers chairs,
And goes around muttering, "nobody cares."
Who fixes charoset and karpas and eggs,
And winds up with headaches and cramps in her legs.
Wouldn't you think that when the matzah is hid,
She merits the prize, not some smart-aleck kid??

- Do we appreciate the roles women play in our lives?
- Are they being expected to play too many roles?
- Can a woman have a career and be a "soccer mom?"
- What path do you think children would want their mothers to take?
- Did you thank the person who made your Seder possible?

בָּרוּךְ הַמָּקוֹם. בָּרוּךְ הוּא. בָּרוּךְ שֶׁנָּתַן תּוֹרָה לְעַמּוֹ יִשְׂרָאֵל. בָּרוּךְ הוּא.

Blessed be the Omnipresent; blessed be He. Blessed be [God] Who has given the Torah to His people Israel; blessed be He.

Arbaa Banim
The Four Children

The Seder and the Haggadah help fulfill the Biblical commandment, *"V'higadta l'vincha* – and you shall tell your children ..." of our Egyptian experience. Years ago King Solomon taught, "Teach your child in the way that he shall understand." To teach and tell the story to our children, we must first understand and accept that all children are different. The Haggadah bases itself on Biblical texts, which relate to four different types of children, "wise," "wicked," "simple," and "the one who does not know how to ask."

The concept of the four children has been put into contemporary terms:

A. Wise – A self-identified personality who constantly wishes to broaden his understanding.
B. Wicked – A negative personality dramatically opposed to just about anything.
C. Simple – A personality characterized by simplistic curiosity.
D. Unable to ask – A personality characterized by indifference.

Which one are you?

Another interpretation sees the four children as really being one and the same. The four are meant to represent the individual at four different stages in the life cycle.

We all start off as the *"sh-eino yodea lishol."* We all begin life as infants unable to ask any questions. All we can really do is cry or make baby talk. It's left to our parents to interpret what's going through our minds and to anticipate all of our needs. We ask no questions, while they provide all the answers.

The next stage in life is that of the *"tam"* -- the simple child, the time in life that is truly "the age of innocence." We're wide-eyed, accepting, learning from parents and teachers, acquiring learning and knowledge, nothing too complex. We ask "What's this?" and we're told, and that's that.

And then comes adolescence - the stage of the *"rasha"*, which we usually translate as "the wicked child", but more appropriate is the "rebellious child." Adolescence is a time of rebellion, a time of confrontation, of challenging authority, a very important and necessary stage in life! *"Mah ha-avodah hazot lachem"* -- What are you people doing? What do you know? Who cares if that's the way it was done in the past? That's why we've got all the problems we've got today. It's time to try something new. The "rebellious stage" is a time of anti-establishment, radical approaches, an alternate lifestyle.

And then comes the fourth stage -- the *"chochom"* -- the adult. He's the one, who by way of experience, has become wise enough to incorporate the new with the old, the radical with values and ideas that have worked for generations. *"Mah ha-edot v'hachukim v'hamishpatim,"* asks the chochom: "What are these laws and statutes and ordinances?" Let me better understand the way the system works. And let me understand what does not work. And let me work within the system to change what needs to be changed, to strengthen what needs to be strengthened.

Four children? No -- just one -- at different stages in life. We all start off as infants asking nothing. But where do we end up? Some of us don't complete the four stages. Some of us suffer from "arrested development." We get stuck at one of the earlier stages and never reach the stage of being the "wise" one.

Do you know anyone like that?

The former Lubavitcher Rebbe, Rabbi Joseph Isaac Schneersohn (1880-1950), is quoted as having seen the four children not as four different children, and not as four different stages of one child's development, but as four different generations of the American experience. As Rabbi Shlomo Riskin phrases it in his commentary to the Haggadah:

The Wise Child represents the European roots, the generation of the grandparents who came to America with beard and earlocks, dressed in shtreimel and kapote, steeped in piety, with a love for learning and profound knowledge of the Jewish tradition.

Their progeny, the Wicked Child, brought up within the American "melting pot," rejected his parent's customs and ways of thought. He thought of himself as being in a new country with new ways of thinking and acting. To him, the parents were terribly old-fashioned and a bit foolish for not immediately adopting the new ways, which seemed more easygoing and profitable. Turning his back on the glories of the Jewish tradition, this child often became successful in business but was cynical in his outlook.

The third generation, the Simple Child, is confused. He watched his grandfather making Kiddush on Friday night and his father standing by silently, perhaps resentfully, impatient to prepare for business on Saturday morning. The memory of this grandfather, though strong at one time, is fading and so the confused Simple Child can only ask, *"mah zot"*, caught as he is in the conflict between his grandfather and his father.

The fourth generation, the Child Who Does Not Know How to Ask, offspring of the Simple Child, is the greatest tragedy of all. He was born after his great-grandparents had died. He knows only his totally assimilated grandfather, the rasha, and his religiously confused father. He does not even know how to ask questions. This is our mute American generation, the generation of the child who thought it was someone's birthday when she saw her great-grandmother lighting the festival candles. The only time this child had seen candles being lit was on birthdays. She did not even know how to ask. We are now being challenged to open our great heritage to this generation which lost it without ever knowing what it had possessed.

There is also a fifth generation, which is merely hinted at in the Haggadah. This generation is so far removed from Judaism that it does not even know it is Passover. No matter what we say about the Wicked Child, at least he is at the Seder. The One Who Does Not Know How to Ask somehow stumbled upon a Seder even if he finds it rather incomprehensible. But that fifth generation in America is not here at all.

• Does this, in some way, describe the generations of your family?

• In some families the process has been reversed with the children becoming more religiously observant than their parents. Is that what you would want in your family?

• Do you see this as causing problems?

• Is there someone at your Seder who is "too" religious?

• What does that mean?

• Can someone be "too" irreligious?

כְּנֶגֶד אַרְבָּעָה בָנִים דִּבְּרָה תוֹרָה. אֶחָד חָכָם, וְאֶחָד רָשָׁע, וְאֶחָד תָּם,
וְאֶחָד שֶׁאֵינוֹ יוֹדֵעַ לִשְׁאוֹל:

חָכָם מַה הוּא אוֹמֵר? מַה הָעֵדוֹת וְהַחֻקִּים וְהַמִּשְׁפָּטִים, אֲשֶׁר צִוָּה יהוה
אֱלֹהֵינוּ אֶתְכֶם? וְאַף אַתָּה אֱמָר לוֹ כְּהִלְכוֹת הַפֶּסַח: אֵין מַפְטִירִין אַחַר
הַפֶּסַח אֲפִיקוֹמָן:

רָשָׁע מַה הוּא אוֹמֵר? מָה הָעֲבוֹדָה הַזֹּאת לָכֶם? לָכֶם וְלֹא לוֹ. וּלְפִי
שֶׁהוֹצִיא אֶת־עַצְמוֹ מִן הַכְּלָל, כָּפַר בָּעִקָּר. וְאַף אַתָּה הַקְהֵה אֶת־שִׁנָּיו,
וֶאֱמָר לוֹ: בַּעֲבוּר זֶה, עָשָׂה יהוה לִי, בְּצֵאתִי מִמִּצְרָיִם, לִי וְלֹא לוֹ. אִלּוּ
הָיָה שָׁם, לֹא הָיָה נִגְאָל:

תָּם מַה הוּא אוֹמֵר? מַה זֹּאת? וְאָמַרְתָּ אֵלָיו: בְּחֹזֶק יָד הוֹצִיאָנוּ יהוה
מִמִּצְרַיִם מִבֵּית עֲבָדִים:

וְשֶׁאֵינוֹ יוֹדֵעַ לִשְׁאוֹל, אַתְּ פְּתַח לוֹ. שֶׁנֶּאֱמַר: וְהִגַּדְתָּ לְבִנְךָ, בַּיּוֹם הַהוּא
לֵאמֹר: בַּעֲבוּר זֶה עָשָׂה יהוה לִי, בְּצֵאתִי מִמִּצְרָיִם:

The Torah refers to four sons; a wise one, and a wicked one, and a simple one, and one who does not know how to ask a question.

The wise son asks: What is the meaning of the testimonies, and the statutes, and the laws which the Lord our God has commanded you? Explain to him the laws of the Pesach: that no dessert may be eaten after the Passover sacrifice.

The wicked son asks: What does this service mean to you? (By the words "to you" he implies that this service is only) for you--not for himself. By excluding himself from the community, he denies the main principle of faith. So tell him bluntly: "This is done on account of what the Lord did for me when I came out of Egypt." For me, not for him; had he been there, he would not have been redeemed.

The simple son asks: What is this? Tell him, "With a strong hand the Lord brought us out of Egypt from the house of slavery."

As for the son who is unable to ask a question, you must open up the subject to him. As it is said: "And you shall tell your son on that day: This is onaccount of what the Lord did for me when I came out of Egypt."

וְהִגַּדְתָּ לְבִנְךָ, יָכוֹל מֵרֹאשׁ חֹדֶשׁ, תַּלְמוּד לוֹמַר "בַּיּוֹם הַהוּא". אִי בַּיּוֹם הַהוּא יָכוֹל מִבְּעוֹד יוֹם? תַּלְמוּד לוֹמַר. "בַּעֲבוּר זֶה". בַּעֲבוּר זֶה לֹא אָמַרְתִּי, אֶלָּא בְּשָׁעָה שֶׁיֵּשׁ מַצָּה וּמָרוֹר מֻנָּחִים לְפָנֶיךָ:

מִתְּחִלָּה עוֹבְדֵי עֲבוֹדָה זָרָה הָיוּ אֲבוֹתֵינוּ. וְעַכְשָׁו קֵרְבָנוּ הַמָּקוֹם לַעֲבוֹדָתוֹ, שֶׁנֶּאֱמַר: וַיֹּאמֶר יְהוֹשֻׁעַ אֶל־כָּל־הָעָם. כֹּה אָמַר יְהוָה אֱלֹהֵי יִשְׂרָאֵל, בְּעֵבֶר הַנָּהָר יָשְׁבוּ אֲבוֹתֵיכֶם מֵעוֹלָם, תֶּרַח אֲבִי אַבְרָהָם וַאֲבִי נָחוֹר. וַיַּעַבְדוּ אֱלֹהִים אֲחֵרִים. וָאֶקַּח אֶת־אֲבִיכֶם אֶת־אַבְרָהָם מֵעֵבֶר הַנָּהָר, וָאוֹלֵךְ אוֹתוֹ בְּכָל־אֶרֶץ כְּנָעַן וָאַרְבֶּה אֶת־זַרְעוֹ, וָאֶתֶּן־לוֹ אֶת־יִצְחָק. וָאֶתֵּן לְיִצְחָק אֶת־יַעֲקֹב וְאֶת־עֵשָׂו. וָאֶתֵּן לְעֵשָׂו אֶת־הַר שֵׂעִיר, לָרֶשֶׁת אוֹתוֹ. וְיַעֲקֹב וּבָנָיו יָרְדוּ מִצְרָיִם:

בָּרוּךְ שׁוֹמֵר הַבְטָחָתוֹ לְיִשְׂרָאֵל. בָּרוּךְ הוּא. שֶׁהַקָּדוֹשׁ בָּרוּךְ הוּא חִשֵּׁב אֶת־הַקֵּץ, לַעֲשׂוֹת כְּמָה שֶׁאָמַר לְאַבְרָהָם אָבִינוּ בִּבְרִית בֵּין הַבְּתָרִים, שֶׁנֶּאֱמַר:

"And you shall tell your son," one might think that the Haggadah should be recited on the first day of the month of Nisan, but the Torah says: "on that day" (the first day of Passover). One might think that the phrase "on that day" means that the story of the Exodus should be recited in the daytime? Therefore, the Torah says: "On account of this." The word "this" refers to the time when this matzah and this marror are placed before you (on Passover night when you are obligated to eat them.)

At first, our forefathers worshiped other gods, but now, the Omnipresent has brought us near to His service, as it is said: "Joshua said to all the people: "So says the Lord, God of Israel--your fathers have always lived beyond the Euphrates River, Terah the father of Abraham and Nahor; they worshipped other gods. I took your father Abraham from the other side of the river and led him through all the land of Canaan. I multiplied his family and gave him Isaac. To Isaac, I gave Jacob and Esau. To Esau, I gave Mount Seir to inherit, however, Jacob and his children went down to Egypt."

Blessed be He Who keeps His promise to Israel; blessed be He. The Holy One, blessed be He, predetermined the time for our final deliverance in order to fulfill what He had pledged to our father Abraham in a covenant, as it is said:

וַיֹּאמֶר לְאַבְרָם יָדֹעַ תֵּדַע, כִּי גֵר יִהְיֶה זַרְעֲךָ, בְּאֶרֶץ לֹא לָהֶם, וַעֲבָדוּם
וְעִנּוּ אֹתָם אַרְבַּע מֵאוֹת שָׁנָה. וְגַם אֶת־הַגּוֹי אֲשֶׁר יַעֲבֹדוּ דָּן אָנֹכִי.
וְאַחֲרֵי כֵן יֵצְאוּ, בִּרְכֻשׁ גָּדוֹל.

The matzot are covered, and the cups are lifted as the following is recited. Upon its conclusion, the cups are put down and the matzot are uncovered.

"He said to Abram, 'You should surely know that your descendants will sojourn in a land that is not their own, and they will be enslaved and afflicted for four hundred years; however, I will judge the nation that enslaved them, and afterwards they shall leave with great wealth.'"

The matzot are covered, and the cups are lifted as the following is recited. Upon its conclusion, the cups are put down and the matzot are uncovered.

V' Hi Sheamdah
And It Is This That Has Stood…

In this prayer a seemingly paranoid statement is made that "not only one nation goes up against us but in every generation they rise up to destroy us." But as has been pointed out, even paranoid people have real enemies. And the fact of the matter is, no people have had more than the Jews!

On March 12, 1992, a powerful car bomb went off outside Israel's embassy in Buenos Aires, Argentina, leveling the embassy to the ground and killing 29 people, wounding 242. Immediately after the attack Argentine President Carlos Menem said publicly that it was most likely carried out by Neo-Nazis. The next day speculation focused on the Islamic Jihad group. Shortly thereafter, it was announced that an international search was on for yet another suspect, a member of the radical German Red Army, Marxist terrorists with close ties to the PLO. Think about it for a minute: what a remarkable people we are. The early 1990's was before Al-Qaeda and the rise of Islamic terrorism. At that time when a bomb went off on the streets of London, everyone knew who did it - the IRA. If it happened in Spain, it was assumed that it was Basque separatists; if in Germany - skinheads; if in Turkey – Kurds. But when it comes to the Jews, it can be anybody and everybody: Argentine Hitler youth, German Marxist revolutionaries, Islamic fanatics, Palestinian terrorists … they all have their own political agendas, some from the left and others from the right. But when it comes to the Jews, they are partners in hatred, some because we're accused of being capitalists, others because we're accused of being communists; some because we're too liberal, others because we're too racist; some because we're too pushy and some because we're too ghettoized; some because we're the chosen people, others because we are an inferior race.

How did we survive when "in every generation they rise up to destroy us"? More than 100 years ago Mark Twain asked this very question when he wrote:

> The Egyptians, the Babylonians and the Persians rose, filled the planet with sound and splendor, then faded to dream-stuff and passed away. The Greeks and the Romans followed and made a vast noise, and they are gone. Other peoples have sprung up and held their torch high for a time but it burned out and they sit in twilight now, or have vanished. The Jew saw them all, survived them all, and is now what he always was; exhibiting no decadence, no infirmities of age, no weakening of his parts, no slowing of his energies, no dulling of his alert and aggressive mind. All things are mortal, but the Jew; all other forces pass but he remains. What is the secret of his immortality?

The *V'hi Sheamdah* concludes by answering this question with the words: "But the Holy One, Blessed be He, always saves us from their hands." It wasn't only the writers of the Haggadah who felt this way. When Fredrich II ("the Great") of Prussia asked his court chaplain for a proof of God's existence, the cleric replied, "Your majesty, the Jews!"

- Do you have a better explanation for the survival of the Jewish people than "it is the will of God?"
- Do you believe God is involved in our daily existence?
- When was the last time your family talked about God?
- Is it possible that He misses you?

וְהִיא שֶׁעָמְדָה לַאֲבוֹתֵינוּ וְלָנוּ. שֶׁלֹּא אֶחָד בִּלְבָד, עָמַד עָלֵינוּ לְכַלּוֹתֵנוּ. אֶלָּא שֶׁבְּכָל־דּוֹר וָדוֹר, עוֹמְדִים עָלֵינוּ לְכַלּוֹתֵנוּ. וְהַקָּדוֹשׁ בָּרוּךְ הוּא מַצִּילֵנוּ מִיָּדָם:

And this promise has sustained our fathers and us. For not only one enemy has risen against us to annihilate us, but in every generation there are those who stand against us to destroy us. But the Holy One, blessed be He, saves us from their hand.

Tzey U'lemad
Go And Learn.

The Mishnah tells us that as part of telling the story of the exodus from Egypt we should focus in particular on four verses: "A wandering Aramean was my father and he went down into Egypt and sojourned there, few in number; and he became there a nation great, mighty and populous. And the Egyptians dealt ill with us, and afflicted us, and laid upon us hard bondage. And we cried unto the Lord, the God of our fathers, and the Lord heard our voice, and saw our affliction and our toil and our oppression. And the Lord brought us forth out of Egypt with a mighty hand, and with an outstretched arm, and with great terribleness and with signs, and with wonders." (Deuteronomy 26:5-8) While these four verses do relate the story of the exodus from Egypt, their choice for special attention in the Haggadah is rather strange. The fact is, when the Temple stood in Jerusalem they were recited not on Pesach but on Shavuot when the *Bikkurim* – "the first fruits" – were brought to the temple. Why on the night of Passover focus on verses from Deuteronomy which were originally intended for Shavuot? Verses from the Book of Exodus would seem to be more appropriate.

While the commentators offer several explanations, perhaps a modern perspective can be noted in the fact that the bringing of the *Bikkurim*, which these verses call to mind, shares something in common with our Passover observance: it can't be done by proxy. As the Haggadah tells us, "Every person is obligated to see himself as if he personally went out of Egypt." The *Bikkurim* ceremony ended with the destruction of the Temple, but the manner in which the ceremony took place still contains a great lesson.

In describing the Bikkurim ritual the Torah tell us: *"V'halachta el ha-makom asher yivchar Hashem Elokecha l'shakein shmo sham* – and you shall go unto the place where the Lord shall choose to cause His name to dwell there." Based on these words, *"V'halachta el ha-makom* – and you shall go unto the place . . ."* Maimonides makes the following comment: "He who brings the first fruits has permission to give them to his servant or relative to carry the whole way until he reaches the outer precincts of the Temple. But when he reaches the outer precincts of the Temple he has to take the basket himself on his own shoulders … even if he be a great king in Israel."

There was just so much your servant, messenger, proxy or personal assistant could do on your behalf. You could delegate responsibility only up to a certain point. You had to bring the *Bikkurim* yourself! You, yourself, had to be there to personally recite the thanksgiving prayer.

This brings to mind Blake Gottesman – a nice Jewish boy. He completed only one year of college, but his job has him spending more time than perhaps anyone else with the most powerful man on earth. Blake Gottesman is the personal assistant to President George Bush. And what are some of the things he does as President Bush's personal assistant? According to *The New York Times*, after President Bush shakes many hands, Mr. Gottesman is there to hand him a hand sanitizer. He also carries along the President's cough drops as well as his magic markers. While Mr. Bush gets his daily intelligence briefing, it is Mr. Gottesman who is taking care of Barney, the President's Scottish terrier. When the President travels, Mr. Gottesman usually has a room next door to him, whether it's in Buckingham Palace or aboard the aircraft carrier Abraham Lincoln.

Would *you* want Mr. Gottesman's job? It depends on how you look at it! On the one hand, on a daily basis he gets to see history being made, a close up view that few ever get. On the other hand, his job can simply be dismissed as being what Jews used to describe in Yiddish as a "shik yingel" – basically a "gofer" who has no independent existence or identity.

Whether you would want to be the President's personal assistant – that's a matter of opinion. But most everyone would like to have a personal assistant, someone who is always there for you, carrying your things, taking care of all the small details, picking up after you, making all the reservations. Many people do have their own personal assistants, people like Itzhak Perlman and rock star Rod Stewart. And many others, like Mick Jagger and Madonna and Paris Hilton, are part of what's called "concierge clubs" or "lifestyle management companies", which book flights for you, make reservations at restaurants and hotels, buy gifts, cars or homes for you, or just get the shopping done and find recipes for dinner parties … all for about $300,000 a year!

Ours is very much a society where people are taught to depend on others to do the work for them.

- We have personal shoppers who pick out our clothing for us.
- We have teachers to educate our children.
- We have maids to clean our homes.
- We have chauffeurs to drive us around.
- We have rabbis to be religious for us.
- We have business managers to balance our books for us.
- There is a service available in Florida where for a fee they will call, send cards and visit your parents in Miami while you are home up North. Yes, there is even a service to be children for us!

But the *Bikkurim* ritual comes to remind us that, as busy as we are, there are certain things that we must do ourselves. No deputy, proxy, messenger or assistant is quite the same. There are certain things that no one can do like you, even if you are a king.

You couldn't have someone else bring the first fruits for you. You can't have someone else "experience" the exodus from Egypt for you.

- Can you have someone else be a child for you?
- Can you have someone else be a parent for you?
- On your list of "things to do" are those the things that you – and you alone – must do?
- Should there be other, more important, "things" on the list?

צֵא וּלְמַד, מַה בִּקֵּשׁ לָבָן הָאֲרַמִּי לַעֲשׂוֹת לְיַעֲקֹב אָבִינוּ. שֶׁפַּרְעֹה לֹא גָזַר אֶלָּא עַל הַזְּכָרִים, וְלָבָן בִּקֵּשׁ לַעֲקוֹר אֶת־הַכֹּל, שֶׁנֶּאֱמַר: אֲרַמִּי אֹבֵד אָבִי, וַיֵּרֶד מִצְרַיְמָה, וַיָּגָר שָׁם בִּמְתֵי מְעָט. וַיְהִי שָׁם לְגוֹי גָּדוֹל, עָצוּם וָרָב.

וַיֵּרֶד מִצְרַיְמָה, אָנוּס עַל פִּי הַדִּבּוּר.

וַיָּגָר שָׁם. מְלַמֵּד שֶׁלֹּא יָרַד יַעֲקֹב אָבִינוּ לְהִשְׁתַּקֵּעַ בְּמִצְרַיִם, אֶלָּא לָגוּר שָׁם, שֶׁנֶּאֱמַר: וַיֹּאמְרוּ אֶל־פַּרְעֹה, לָגוּר בָּאָרֶץ בָּאנוּ, כִּי־אֵין מִרְעֶה לַצֹּאן אֲשֶׁר לַעֲבָדֶיךָ, כִּי כָבֵד הָרָעָב בְּאֶרֶץ כְּנָעַן. וְעַתָּה, יֵשְׁבוּ־נָא עֲבָדֶיךָ בְּאֶרֶץ גֹּשֶׁן:

בִּמְתֵי מְעָט. כְּמָה שֶׁנֶּאֱמַר: בְּשִׁבְעִים נֶפֶשׁ, יָרְדוּ אֲבֹתֶיךָ מִצְרַיְמָה. וְעַתָּה, שָׂמְךָ יְהוָה אֱלֹהֶיךָ, כְּכוֹכְבֵי הַשָּׁמַיִם לָרֹב.

וַיְהִי שָׁם לְגוֹי. מְלַמֵּד שֶׁהָיוּ יִשְׂרָאֵל מְצֻיָּנִין שָׁם:

גָּדוֹל עָצוּם, כְּמָה שֶׁנֶּאֱמַר: וּבְנֵי יִשְׂרָאֵל, פָּרוּ וַיִּשְׁרְצוּ, וַיִּרְבּוּ וַיַּעַצְמוּ, בִּמְאֹד מְאֹד, וַתִּמָּלֵא הָאָרֶץ אֹתָם:

Go and learn what Lavan the Aramean tried to do to our father, Jacob. While Pharaoh decreed only against the male children, Lavan tried to uproot us all, as it is said: "An Aramaean sought to destroy my father, however, he went down to Egypt and sojourned there few in number and there he became a great, mighty, and numerous nation."

He went down to Egypt, compelled by Divine decree.

He sojourned there, implies that he did not come down to settle in Egypt, but only to live there temporarily, as it is said: "They (the sons of Jacob) said to Pharaoh: 'We have come to sojourn in this land because there is no pasture for your servants' flocks, for the famine is severe in the land of Canaan. For now, though, let your servants dwell in the land of Goshen.'"

Few in number, as it is said: "With seventy souls your ancestors went down to Egypt, and now the Lord your God has made you as numerous as the stars in the sky."

There he became a nation teaches that they became a distinct people in Egypt.

Great, mighty, as it is said: "The children of Israel were fruitful and increased greatly; and they multiplied and they became mighty, and the land was full of them."

וָרָב. כְּמָה שֶׁנֶּאֱמַר: רְבָבָה כְּצֶמַח הַשָּׂדֶה נְתַתִּיךָ, וַתִּרְבִּי, וַתִּגְדְּלִי, וַתָּבֹאִי בַּעֲדִי עֲדָיִים: שָׁדַיִם נָכֹנוּ, וּשְׂעָרֵךְ צִמֵּחַ, וְאַתְּ עֵרֹם וְעֶרְיָה:

וָאֶעֱבֹר עָלַיִךְ וָאֶרְאֵךְ מִתְבּוֹסֶסֶת בְּדָמָיִךְ וָאֹמַר לָךְ בְּדָמַיִךְ חֲיִי וָאֹמַר לָךְ בְּדָמַיִךְ חֲיִי.

וַיָּרֵעוּ אֹתָנוּ הַמִּצְרִים וַיְעַנּוּנוּ. וַיִּתְּנוּ עָלֵינוּ עֲבֹדָה קָשָׁה.

וַיָּרֵעוּ אֹתָנוּ הַמִּצְרִים. כְּמָה שֶׁנֶּאֱמַר: הָבָה נִתְחַכְּמָה לוֹ. פֶּן יִרְבֶּה, וְהָיָה כִּי תִקְרֶאנָה מִלְחָמָה, וְנוֹסַף גַּם-הוּא עַל-שֹׂנְאֵינוּ, וְנִלְחַם-בָּנוּ וְעָלָה מִן-הָאָרֶץ:

וַיְעַנּוּנוּ. כְּמָה שֶׁנֶּאֱמַר: וַיָּשִׂימוּ עָלָיו שָׂרֵי מִסִּים, לְמַעַן עַנֹּתוֹ בְּסִבְלֹתָם: וַיִּבֶן עָרֵי מִסְכְּנוֹת לְפַרְעֹה, אֶת פִּתֹם וְאֶת רַעַמְסֵס.

וַיִּתְּנוּ עָלֵינוּ עֲבֹדָה קָשָׁה. כְּמָה שֶׁנֶּאֱמַר: וַיַּעֲבִדוּ מִצְרַיִם אֶת-בְּנֵי יִשְׂרָאֵל בְּפָרֶךְ:

And numerous, as it is said: "I made you as numerous as the plants of the field; you increased and grew, and came to have great beauty; your breasts were firm and your hair grew long; and yet, you were bare and naked."

I passed over you and saw you downtrodden in your blood and I said to you: "Through your blood you shall live!" And I said to you: "Through your blood you shall live."

"And the Egyptians dealt cruelly with us and afflicted us; and they imposed hard labor upon us."

And the Egyptians dealt cruelly with us, as it is said: "Let us deal with them wisely lest they multiply, and, if we happen to be at war, and they may join our enemies and fight against us and then leave the country."

And afflicted us, as it is said: "They set taskmasters over them in order to oppress them with their burdens; and they built Pitom and Raamses as store cities for Pharaoh."

And they imposed hard labor upon us, as it is said: "And they imposed back breaking labor upon the people of Israel."

וַנִּצְעַק אֶל־יהוה אֱלֹהֵי אֲבֹתֵינוּ, וַיִּשְׁמַע יהוה אֶת־קֹלֵנוּ, וַיַּרְא אֶת־עָנְיֵנוּ, וְאֶת־עֲמָלֵנוּ, וְאֶת לַחֲצֵנוּ.

וַנִּצְעַק אֶל־יהוה אֱלֹהֵי אֲבֹתֵינוּ, כְּמָה שֶׁנֶּאֱמַר: וַיְהִי בַיָּמִים הָרַבִּים הָהֵם, וַיָּמָת מֶלֶךְ מִצְרַיִם, וַיֵּאָנְחוּ בְנֵי־יִשְׂרָאֵל מִן־הָעֲבֹדָה וַיִּזְעָקוּ. וַתַּעַל שַׁוְעָתָם אֶל־הָאֱלֹהִים מִן־הָעֲבֹדָה:

וַיִּשְׁמַע יהוה אֶת־קֹלֵנוּ. כְּמָה שֶׁנֶּאֱמַר: וַיִּשְׁמַע אֱלֹהִים אֶת־נַאֲקָתָם, וַיִּזְכֹּר אֱלֹהִים אֶת־בְּרִיתוֹ, אֶת־אַבְרָהָם, אֶת־יִצְחָק, וְאֶת־יַעֲקֹב:

וַיַּרְא אֶת־עָנְיֵנוּ. זוֹ פְּרִישׁוּת דֶּרֶךְ אֶרֶץ. כְּמָה שֶׁנֶּאֱמַר: וַיַּרְא אֱלֹהִים אֶת־בְּנֵי יִשְׂרָאֵל. וַיֵּדַע אֱלֹהִים:

וְאֶת־עֲמָלֵנוּ. אֵלּוּ הַבָּנִים. כְּמָה שֶׁנֶּאֱמַר: כָּל־הַבֵּן הַיִּלּוֹד הַיְאֹרָה תַּשְׁלִיכֻהוּ, וְכָל־הַבַּת תְּחַיּוּן:

וְאֶת לַחֲצֵנוּ. זֶה הַדְּחַק. כְּמָה שֶׁנֶּאֱמַר: וְגַם־רָאִיתִי אֶת־הַלַּחַץ, אֲשֶׁר מִצְרַיִם לֹחֲצִים אֹתָם:

"And we cried to the Lord, the God of our fathers; and the Lord heard our cry and saw our affliction, and our toil, and our oppression."

And we cried to the Lord, the God of our fathers, as it is said: "And it happened in the course of those many days that the king of Egypt died; and the children of Israel sighed because of their labor and cried; and their cry went up to God from their labor."

And the Lord heard our cry, as it is said: "And God heard their groaning; and God remembered His covenant with Abraham, with Isaac, and with Jacob."

And saw our affliction, that is the conjugal separation of husband and wife, as it is said: "And God saw the children of Israel and God knew."

And our toil refers to the drowning of the sons, as it is said: "Every son that is born you shall cast into the river, but you shall let every daughter live."

And our oppression, means the pressure used upon them, as it is said: "And I have also seen the oppression with which Egypt is oppressing them."

וַיּוֹצִאֵנוּ יהוה מִמִּצְרַיִם, בְּיָד חֲזָקָה, וּבִזְרֹעַ נְטוּיָה, וּבְמֹרָא גָּדֹל וּבְאֹתוֹת וּבְמֹפְתִים:

וַיּוֹצִאֵנוּ יהוה מִמִּצְרַיִם. לֹא עַל יְדֵי מַלְאָךְ, וְלֹא עַל־יְדֵי שָׂרָף, וְלֹא עַל־יְדֵי שָׁלִיחַ. אֶלָּא הַקָּדוֹשׁ בָּרוּךְ הוּא בִּכְבוֹדוֹ וּבְעַצְמוֹ. שֶׁנֶּאֱמַר: וְעָבַרְתִּי בְאֶרֶץ־מִצְרַיִם בַּלַּיְלָה הַזֶּה, וְהִכֵּיתִי כָל־בְּכוֹר בְּאֶרֶץ מִצְרַיִם, מֵאָדָם וְעַד־בְּהֵמָה, וּבְכָל־אֱלֹהֵי מִצְרַיִם אֶעֱשֶׂה שְׁפָטִים אֲנִי יהוה:

וְעָבַרְתִּי בְאֶרֶץ־מִצְרַיִם. אֲנִי וְלֹא מַלְאָךְ. וְהִכֵּיתִי כָל בְּכוֹר. אֲנִי וְלֹא שָׂרָף. וּבְכָל־אֱלֹהֵי מִצְרַיִם אֶעֱשֶׂה שְׁפָטִים. אֲנִי וְלֹא הַשָּׁלִיחַ. אֲנִי יהוה. אֲנִי הוּא וְלֹא אַחֵר:

בְּיָד חֲזָקָה. זוֹ הַדֶּבֶר. כְּמָה שֶׁנֶּאֱמַר: הִנֵּה יַד־יהוה הוֹיָה, בְּמִקְנְךָ אֲשֶׁר בַּשָּׂדֶה, בַּסּוּסִים בַּחֲמֹרִים בַּגְּמַלִּים, בַּבָּקָר וּבַצֹּאן, דֶּבֶר כָּבֵד מְאֹד:

"And the Lord brought us out of Egypt with a mighty hand and with an outstretched arm, and with great awe, and with miraculous signs and with wonders."

The Lord brought us out of Egypt, not by an angel, and not by a seraph, and not by a messenger, but the Holy One, blessed be He, Himself, and in His glory as it is said: "For I will pass through the land of Egypt on that night; and I will smite all the firstborn in the land of Egypt from man unto beast; and on all the gods of Egypt I will execute judgments; I am the Lord."

(Explain this as follows:)

And I will pass through the land of Egypt, Myself and not an angel; And I will smite all the firstborn, Myself and not a seraph; and on all the gods of Egypt I will execute judgments, Myself and not a messenger; I am the Lord, I am and none other.

With a mighty hand, refers to the disease among the cattle, as it is said: "Behold the hand of the Lord strikes your cattle which are in the field, the horses, the donkeys, the camels, the herds, and the flocks - a very severe pestilence."

And with great awe, alludes to the divine revelation, as it is said: "Or has God ever attempted to take unto Himself, a nation from the midst of another nation, by trials, by miraculous signs and with wonders, and by war and with a mighty hand and with an outstretched arm and by awesome revelations,

וּבִזְרֹעַ נְטוּיָה. זוֹ הַחֶרֶב. כְּמָה שֶׁנֶּאֱמַר: וְחַרְבּוֹ שְׁלוּפָה בְּיָדוֹ, נְטוּיָה עַל יְרוּשָׁלָיִם:

וּבְמֹרָא גָּדֹל, זֶה גִּלּוּי שְׁכִינָה. כְּמָה שֶׁנֶּאֱמַר: אוֹ הֲנִסָּה אֱלֹהִים, לָבוֹא לָקַחַת לוֹ גוֹי מִקֶּרֶב גּוֹי, בְּמַסֹּת בְּאֹתֹת וּבְמוֹפְתִים וּבְמִלְחָמָה, וּבְיָד חֲזָקָה וּבִזְרֹעַ נְטוּיָה, וּבְמוֹרָאִים גְּדֹלִים. כְּכֹל אֲשֶׁר־עָשָׂה לָכֶם יְהוָה אֱלֹהֵיכֶם בְּמִצְרַיִם, לְעֵינֶיךָ:

וּבְאֹתוֹת. זֶה הַמַּטֶּה, כְּמָה שֶׁנֶּאֱמַר: וְאֶת־הַמַּטֶּה הַזֶּה תִּקַּח בְּיָדֶךָ. אֲשֶׁר תַּעֲשֶׂה־בּוֹ אֶת־הָאֹתֹת:

וּבְמֹפְתִים. זֶה הַדָּם. כְּמָה שֶׁנֶּאֱמַר: וְנָתַתִּי מוֹפְתִים, בַּשָּׁמַיִם וּבָאָרֶץ.

As each of the following words is recited, a drop of wine is removed from the cup using a finger, a utensil, or by tilting the cup.

דָּם. וָאֵשׁ. וְתִימְרוֹת עָשָׁן:

דָּבָר אַחֵר. בְּיָד חֲזָקָה שְׁתַּיִם. וּבִזְרֹעַ נְטוּיָה שְׁתַּיִם. וּבְמֹרָא גָּדֹל שְׁתַּיִם. וּבְאֹתוֹת שְׁתַּיִם. וּבְמֹפְתִים שְׁתַּיִם:

---

just as you all saw the Lord your God do for you in Egypt, before your eyes?"

And with miraculous signs, refers to the miracles performed with the staff (of Moses), as it is said: "And take this staff in your hand, that you may perform the miraculous signs with it."

And with wonders, alludes to the blood, as it is said: "And I will show wonders in the heavens and on the earth."

As each of the following words is recited, a drop of wine is removed from the cup using a finger, a utensil, or by tilting the cup.

Blood, Fire, & Pillars of Smoke

Another explanation is: (Each two-word phrase represents two plagues, hence) strong hand, two: outstretched arm, two: great awe, two: miraculous signs, two; wonders, two.

THE TEN PLAGUES

After thousands of years of being in the background, Kabbalah has made it to the front pages ... and all because of Madonna! Madonna has put Kabbalah on the map. Kabbalah has become the "hit" of Hollywood. You don't have to be Jewish to love Kabbalah. Mick Jagger, Rosie O'Donnell, Marla Maples, Demi Moore, Guy Ritchie, Courtney Love and the great mystics, Britney Spears and Mike Tyson ... they and so many others have been attracted to Kabbalah. Madonna, the best-known mystical disciple, is the woman who became famous by simulating sex in front of teenagers on MTV and whose vulgar displays include kissing Britney Spears on stage and going naked in her films. She does not have a clue about what Kabbalah is, if she could say – as she has – "I think Kabbalah is very punk rock." No, it's not!

Kabbalah is based on the idea that God is the *Ein Sof*, which means "without boundaries." As the *Ein Sof*, God is inaccessible and unknowable. However, God does make the Divine Self known through a series of ten *Sefirot*, or emanations from His Divine light. It is through these spheres that the individual can make contact with God. For the Kabbalists it was only natural (or supernatural) that when God wants to have His presence made manifest in this world – for better or for worse – it should be through the number 10. And that's just what we find with the ten plagues and the Ten Commandments, something that Rabbi Benjamin Blech refers to as "the ten-ten principle."

When God appoints Moses to be the leader of the Jewish people, He tells Moses to stand before Pharaoh and tell him that he is speaking in the name of *"Hashem Elokay ha-ivriim* – the Lord, the God of the Hebrews." The word for "Hebrews" is *"ivrim."* In every other place in the Bible where this word is used it is spelled with one *"yud"* but here it is spelled *"ivriim,"* with two *yuds*. Interestingly, the Hebrew letter *"yud"* has the numeric value of 10 ... leading one great Biblical commentator to point out that God is directing Moses to tell Pharaoh that he is speaking in the name of a God who is capable of bringing two yuds – two 10's – either the ten plagues or the Ten Commandments. It is now up to

Pharaoh to decide whether he will choose to follow the principles of the Ten Commandments, thereby sparing the Egyptian people, or if he will choose a path of cruelty, enslavement and immorality, thereby inflicting upon them the ten plagues that will inevitably follow.

Ten plagues and Ten Commandments are not just a coincidence. It is part of a divine plan and a Biblical concept: the ten-ten principle. There are things in this world that are parallel to each other which explain to us in life WHY things happen: the ten-ten principle. Why the ten plagues? Because of the rejection of the lessons of the Ten Commandments. And according to the Kabbalists, one aspect of the physical makeup of our bodies reminds us of this all-important principle each day of our lives. We come into this world with a body that has on it ten fingers – not eight, not twelve … just ten. Is this just part of a random evolutionary process? Simple coincidence? Not to the Kabbalists. To their way of thinking, God put ten fingers on the human body so that each and every day we would all have staring in our faces the ten-ten principle, reminding us that our lives are to be conducted by the moral and ethical lessons of the Ten Commandments, for if not, our lives would be haunted by the ten plagues.

- Do you think God gave us ten fingers for this reason?
- Do you think it was God who gave us ten fingers?
- Where do you stand on the Creation vs. Evolution debate?
- Is it possible there is some truth to both sides?
- And what do you think of Kabbalah … what do you think of Madonna?

אֵלּוּ עֶשֶׂר מַכּוֹת שֶׁהֵבִיא הַקָּדוֹשׁ בָּרוּךְ הוּא עַל הַמִּצְרִים בְּמִצְרַיִם,
וְאֵלּוּ הֵן:

As each of the plagues is recited, a drop of wine is removed from the cup using a finger, a utensil, or by tilting the cup.

דָּם • צְפַרְדֵּעַ • כִּנִּים • עָרוֹב • דֶּבֶר • שְׁחִין • בָּרָד • אַרְבֶּה • חֹשֶׁךְ • מַכַּת בְּכוֹרוֹת:

רַבִּי יְהוּדָה הָיָה נוֹתֵן בָּהֶם סִמָּנִים:

דְּצַ"ךְ עֲדַ"שׁ בְּאַחַ"ב:

The cups are refilled.

רַבִּי יוֹסֵי הַגְּלִילִי אוֹמֵר: מִנַּיִן אַתָּה אוֹמֵר, שֶׁלָּקוּ הַמִּצְרִים בְּמִצְרַיִם עֶשֶׂר מַכּוֹת, וְעַל הַיָּם, לָקוּ חֲמִשִּׁים מַכּוֹת? בְּמִצְרַיִם מָה הוּא אוֹמֵר: וַיֹּאמְרוּ הַחַרְטֻמִּים אֶל פַּרְעֹה, אֶצְבַּע אֱלֹהִים הִיא. וְעַל הַיָּם מָה הוּא אוֹמֵר? וַיַּרְא יִשְׂרָאֵל אֶת הַיָּד הַגְּדֹלָה, אֲשֶׁר עָשָׂה יהוה בְּמִצְרַיִם, וַיִּרְאוּ הָעָם אֶת יהוה. וַיַּאֲמִינוּ בַּיהוה, וּבְמֹשֶׁה עַבְדּוֹ. כַּמָּה לָקוּ בָאֶצְבַּע, עֶשֶׂר מַכּוֹת: אֱמוֹר מֵעַתָּה, בְּמִצְרַיִם לָקוּ עֶשֶׂר מַכּוֹת, וְעַל־הַיָּם, לָקוּ חֲמִשִּׁים מַכּוֹת:

These are the ten plagues which the Holy One, blessed be He, brought upon the Egyptians in Egypt, and they are:

As each of the plagues is recited, a drop of wine is removed from the cup using a finger, a utensil, or by tilting the cup.

Blood • Frogs • Vermin • Beasts • Cattle Disease • Boils
Hail • Locusts • Darkness • Slaying of the First Born

Rabbi Yehuda abbreviated the Ten Plagues by composing three words from their Hebrew initials:

D'tzach, A'dash, B'achav

The cups are refilled.

Rabbi Yose the Galilean says: How does one derive that, after the ten plagues in Egypt, the Egyptians suffered fifty plagues at the Sea? Concerning the plagues in Egypt what does the Torah state? "And the magicians said to Pharaoh, it is the finger of God." At the Sea, what does the Torah relate? "And Israel saw the great hand which the Lord laid upon the Egyptians, and the people revered the Lord and they believed in the Lord and in His servant Moses." How many were they struck with by the one finger? Ten. One may reason that if they suffered ten plagues in Egypt, they must have been made to suffer fifty plagues at the Sea.

רַבִּי אֱלִיעֶזֶר אוֹמֵר: מִנַּיִן שֶׁכָּל־מַכָּה וּמַכָּה, שֶׁהֵבִיא הַקָּדוֹשׁ בָּרוּךְ הוּא עַל הַמִּצְרִים בְּמִצְרַיִם, הָיְתָה שֶׁל אַרְבַּע מַכּוֹת? שֶׁנֶּאֱמַר: יְשַׁלַּח בָּם חֲרוֹן אַפּוֹ, עֶבְרָה וָזַעַם וְצָרָה, מִשְׁלַחַת מַלְאֲכֵי רָעִים. עֶבְרָה אַחַת. וָזַעַם שְׁתַּיִם. וְצָרָה שָׁלשׁ. מִשְׁלַחַת מַלְאֲכֵי רָעִים אַרְבַּע: אֱמוֹר מֵעַתָּה, בְּמִצְרַיִם לָקוּ אַרְבָּעִים מַכּוֹת, וְעַל הַיָּם לָקוּ מָאתַיִם מַכּוֹת:

רַבִּי עֲקִיבָא אוֹמֵר: מִנַּיִן שֶׁכָּל מַכָּה וּמַכָּה, שֶׁהֵבִיא הַקָּדוֹשׁ בָּרוּךְ הוּא עַל הַמִּצְרִים בְּמִצְרַיִם, הָיְתָה שֶׁל חָמֵשׁ מַכּוֹת? שֶׁנֶּאֱמַר: יְשַׁלַּח בָּם חֲרוֹן אַפּוֹ, עֶבְרָה וָזַעַם וְצָרָה, מִשְׁלַחַת מַלְאֲכֵי רָעִים. חֲרוֹן אַפּוֹ אַחַת. עֶבְרָה שְׁתַּיִם. וָזַעַם שָׁלשׁ. וְצָרָה אַרְבַּע. מִשְׁלַחַת מַלְאֲכֵי רָעִים חָמֵשׁ. אֱמוֹר מֵעַתָּה, בְּמִצְרַיִם לָקוּ חֲמִשִּׁים מַכּוֹת, וְעַל הַיָּם לָקוּ חֲמִשִּׁים וּמָאתַיִם מַכּוֹת:

Rabbi Eliezer says: How does one derive that every plague that God inflicted upon the Egyptians in Egypt was equal in intensity to four plagues? It says: "He sent upon them His fierce anger: wrath, and fury, and trouble, a band of evil messengers." Since each plague was comprised of 1) wrath, 2) fury, 3) trouble, and 4) a band of evil messengers, one may reason that they must have suffered forty plagues in Egypt and two hundred at the Sea.

Rabbi Akiva says: How does one derive that every plague that God inflicted upon the Egyptians in Egypt was equal in intensity to five plagues? It says: "He sent upon them His fierce anger, wrath, and fury, and trouble, a band of evil messengers." Since each plague was comprised of 1) fierce anger, 2) wrath, 3) fury, 4) trouble, and 5) a band of evil messengers, one may reason that they must have suffered fifty plagues in Egypt and two hundred and fifty at the Sea.

DAYENU

The song "Dayenu" is the most popular one at the Seder. Along with "Havah Negilah," it is the most popular of all Jewish tunes. But there is more to this song than meets the eye. It speaks of the Jews' sense of gratitude for all that God did for us, beginning with the exodus from Egypt and bringing us all the way to the land of Israel. We don't know when the Dayenu was written; we do know that it first appears in a 10th century prayer book of Saadiah Gaon as an optional addition to the Haggadah, and we know Maimonides doesn't include it in his Haggadah. The truth is, what we say in Dayenu is really not true! This expression of gratitude was not the way our ancestors reacted to all the miracles that God did for us at the time of the exodus. Indeed, the Psalmist bitterly criticized how the Jews acted then.

> How oft did they rebel against Him in the wilderness,
> And grieve Him in the desert!
> And still again they tried God,
> And set bounds to the Holy One of Israel.
> They remembered not His hand,
> Nor the day when He redeemed them from the adversary.
> How He set His signs in Egypt and His wonders in the field of Zoan.
> And they turned their rivers into blood, so that they could not drink their streams.
>
> Psalms 78:40-44

You know who took note of this fact? The early Christians who used this to underscore why God had to make a new covenant with the Jewish people and brought Jesus into this world. One of the earliest Christian writers was Melito, the Bishop of Sardis, who wrote in the last half of the 2nd century. Many of his writings have disappeared, but not the composition entitled, "About Easter."

Israel the ungrateful …

How much did you value the ten plagues?
How much did you value the nightly pillar and the daily cloud,
And the crossing of the Red Sea?
How much did you value the giving of manna from heaven,
and the supply of water from a rock, and the giving of Torah at
Horeb, and the inheritance of the Land?

Melito of Sardis, About Easter

Does that language sound familiar? Is it not the flip side of the Dayenu?
Was the Dayenu written as a response to it? There is no way of knowing
for sure but one thing is certain: it sounds a lot better than the words
someone claims he found in a Haggadah discovered in the wilderness
somewhere between Egypt and the Promised Land. It is called "The
Kvetcher's Haggadah." It reads in part:

> "If He had just brought us out of Egypt, and not made
> us shlep all of their wealth . . . that would have been bad
> enough.
>
> If He had made us schlep all their wealth, and had not
> frightened us half to death at the Red Sea . . . before the
> water finally split . . . that would have been bad enough.
>
> If He had frightened us half to death at the Red Sea . . .
> and not made us schlep through the desert for 40 years,
> that would have been bad enough.
>
> If He had made us schlep through the desert for 40
> years and not made us eat the manna, which tasted like
> cardboard . . . that would have been bad enough."

• What kind of person are you – the one who sings
Dayenu in gratitude to God, or the one who wallows in
the Kvetcher's Haggadah?
• Is there someone at your Seder who only sees his cup as
"half full?"
• Is there enough wine in the world to fill it?

כַּמָּה מַעֲלוֹת טוֹבוֹת לַמָּקוֹם עָלֵינוּ׃

אִלּוּ הוֹצִיאָנוּ מִמִּצְרַיִם,
וְלֹא עָשָׂה בָהֶם שְׁפָטִים, דַּיֵּנוּ׃

אִלּוּ עָשָׂה בָהֶם שְׁפָטִים,
וְלֹא עָשָׂה בֵאלֹהֵיהֶם, דַּיֵּנוּ׃

אִלּוּ עָשָׂה בֵאלֹהֵיהֶם,
וְלֹא הָרַג אֶת בְּכוֹרֵיהֶם, דַּיֵּנוּ׃

אִלּוּ הָרַג אֶת בְּכוֹרֵיהֶם,
וְלֹא נָתַן לָנוּ אֶת מָמוֹנָם, דַּיֵּנוּ׃

אִלּוּ נָתַן לָנוּ אֶת מָמוֹנָם,
וְלֹא קָרַע לָנוּ אֶת הַיָּם, דַּיֵּנוּ׃

אִלּוּ קָרַע לָנוּ אֶת הַיָּם,
וְלֹא הֶעֱבִירָנוּ בְתוֹכוֹ בֶּחָרָבָה דַּיֵּנוּ׃

אִלּוּ הֶעֱבִירָנוּ בְתוֹכוֹ בֶּחָרָבָה,
וְלֹא שִׁקַּע צָרֵינוּ בְּתוֹכוֹ, דַּיֵּנוּ׃

How many are the favors which the Omnipresent has bestowed upon us!

Had He brought us out of Egypt, and not executed judgments against the Egyptians, it would have been sufficient for us - Dayenu

Had He executed judgments against the Egyptians, and not their gods, it would have been sufficient for us - Dayenu

Had He executed judgments against their gods and not killed their firstborn, it would have been sufficient for us - Dayenu

Had He put to death their firstborn, and not given us their wealth, it would have been sufficient for us - Dayenu

Had He given us their wealth, and not split the sea for us, it would have been sufficient for us - Dayenu

Had He split the sea for us, and not led us through it on dry land, it would have been sufficient for us - Dayenu

Had He led us through it on dry land, and not sunk our foes in it, it would have been sufficient for us - Dayenu

אִלּוּ שִׁקַּע צָרֵינוּ בְּתוֹכוֹ,

וְלֹא סִפֵּק צָרְכֵּינוּ בַּמִּדְבָּר אַרְבָּעִים שָׁנָה,   דַּיֵּנוּ:

אִלּוּ סִפֵּק צָרְכֵּינוּ בַּמִּדְבָּר אַרְבָּעִים שָׁנָה,

וְלֹא הֶאֱכִילָנוּ אֶת הַמָּן,   דַּיֵּנוּ:

אִלּוּ הֶאֱכִילָנוּ אֶת הַמָּן,

וְלֹא נָתַן לָנוּ אֶת הַשַּׁבָּת,   דַּיֵּנוּ:

אִלּוּ נָתַן לָנוּ אֶת הַשַּׁבָּת,

וְלֹא קֵרְבָנוּ לִפְנֵי הַר סִינַי,   דַּיֵּנוּ:

אִלּוּ קֵרְבָנוּ לִפְנֵי הַר סִינַי,

וְלֹא נָתַן לָנוּ אֶת הַתּוֹרָה,   דַּיֵּנוּ:

אִלּוּ נָתַן לָנוּ אֶת הַתּוֹרָה,

וְלֹא הִכְנִיסָנוּ לְאֶרֶץ יִשְׂרָאֵל,   דַּיֵּנוּ:

אִלּוּ הִכְנִיסָנוּ לְאֶרֶץ יִשְׂרָאֵל,

וְלֹא בָנָה לָנוּ אֶת־בֵּית הַבְּחִירָה,   דַּיֵּנוּ:

Had He sunk our foes in it, and not satisfied our needs in the desert for forty years, it would have been sufficient for us - Dayenu

Had He satisfied our needs in the desert for forty years, and not fed us the manna, it would have been sufficient for us - Dayenu

Had He fed us the manna, and not given us the Sabbath, it would have been sufficient for us - Dayenu

Had He given us the Sabbath, and not brought us to Mount Sinai, it would have been sufficient for us - Dayenu

Had He brought us to Mount Sinai, and not given us the Torah, it would have been sufficient for us - Dayenu

Had He given us the Torah, and not brought us into the land of Israel, it would have been sufficient for us - Dayenu

Had He brought us into the land of Israel, and not built the Temple for us, it would have been sufficient for us - Dayenu

עַל אַחַת כַּמָּה וְכַמָּה טוֹבָה כְפוּלָה וּמְכֻפֶּלֶת לַמָּקוֹם עָלֵינוּ:
שֶׁהוֹצִיאָנוּ מִמִּצְרַיִם,
וְעָשָׂה בָהֶם שְׁפָטִים,
וְעָשָׂה בֵאלֹהֵיהֶם,
וְהָרַג אֶת בְּכוֹרֵיהֶם,
וְנָתַן לָנוּ אֶת־מָמוֹנָם,
וְקָרַע לָנוּ אֶת־הַיָּם,
וְהֶעֱבִירָנוּ בְתוֹכוֹ בֶּחָרָבָה,
וְשִׁקַּע צָרֵינוּ בְּתוֹכוֹ,
וְסִפֵּק צָרְכֵּנוּ בַּמִּדְבָּר אַרְבָּעִים שָׁנָה,
וְהֶאֱכִילָנוּ אֶת־הַמָּן,
וְנָתַן לָנוּ אֶת־הַשַּׁבָּת,
וְקֵרְבָנוּ לִפְנֵי הַר סִינַי,
וְנָתַן לָנוּ אֶת־הַתּוֹרָה,
וְהִכְנִיסָנוּ לְאֶרֶץ יִשְׂרָאֵל,
וּבָנָה לָנוּ אֶת־בֵּית הַבְּחִירָה לְכַפֵּר עַל כָּל־עֲוֹנוֹתֵינוּ.

How much more so, then should we be grateful to God for the numerous favors that the Omnipresent bestowed upon us:

That He brought us out of Egypt,

and punished the Egyptians;

And smote their gods,

and slew their firstborns;

And gave us their wealth,

and split the sea for us;

And led us through it on dry land,

and sunk our foes in it;

And sustained us in the desert for forty years,

and fed us with the manna;

And gave us the Sabbath,

and brought us to Mount Sinai;

And gave us the Torah,

and brought us to the land of Israel;

And built the Temple for us to atone for all our sins.

PESACH, MATZAH U'MAROR

Rabbi Gamliel says, "Whoever does not speak of the following three things on Pesach has not fulfilled his duty: the Pesach sacrifice, matzah and maror." On a simple level, Rabbi Gamliel is telling us that these three items are central to our reliving the Egyptian experience. But this is strange. There is no other commandment like this. There is no other mitzvah whose fulfillment is predicated on an initial explanation of its significance. We are never told that we had to explain the reason for the lulav and etrog on Sukkot or the shofar on Rosh Hashana. So why is Rabbi Gamliel so insistent that without such a public explanation one does not even fulfill the mitzvah of Pesach, matzah and maror?

Israel Yuval, professor of medieval Jewish history at the Hebrew University in Jerusalem, provides an answer to this question that has contemporary relevance. Rabbi Gamliel lived during the second century when Christianity was first developing. This was at a time when the Hebrew Christians were rewriting their Haggadah and for them the concept of Pesach, matzah and maror took on new meaning. The early Christians put a new "spin" on our ancient rituals. Their interpretation of what the symbols of the Seder represent can be found on a web page: www.GodandScience.org. where we are told:

> The original celebration centered around the Passover lamb, which was sacrificed and its blood put over the doorposts as a sign of faith, so that the Lord passed over the houses of the Jews during the last plague poured out on the Egyptians – the killing of every firstborn. To a large degree, the Passover lamb has been eliminated from the Passover festival (with the only remnant being the roasted lamb shank bone). The New Testament says that Jesus is our sacrificial lamb. The Passover lamb was to be a 'male without defect', which is the same description given to Jesus. In addition, when the lamb was roasted and eaten, none of its bones were to be broken. This fact

was also prophesized for the Messiah, whose bones were not to be broken.

Three matzahs are put together (representing the Father, Son and Holy Spirit). The middle matzah is broken, wrapped in a white cloth and hidden, representing the death and burial of Jesus. The matzah itself is designed to represent Jesus, since it is striped and pierced, which was prophesized by Isaiah, David and Zechariah. Following the Seder meal, the 'buried' matzah is 'resurrected', which was foretold in the prophecies of David.

Rabbi Gamliel was very aware of the threat the Hebrew Christians were bringing by their reinterpretation of Jewish tradition. His statement commands us to understand fully the true meaning of the Pesach, matzah and maror which became central to the proper way of observing Pesach. That was his way of making sure that our narrative would not be rewritten.

- In our day many churches are conducting a Seder, associating it with Jesus' "last supper." Is this good for the Jews?
- If Jewish children were given a Christian Haggadah, would they know the difference?
- Do you consider a "Jew for Jesus" a Jew?
- Is Jesus as Messiah the only difference between Judaism and Christianity?
- Do you believe in the "coming of the Messiah"?

רַבָּן גַּמְלִיאֵל הָיָה אוֹמֵר: כָּל־שֶׁלֹּא אָמַר שְׁלֹשָׁה דְבָרִים אֵלּוּ בַּפֶּסַח, לֹא יָצָא יְדֵי חוֹבָתוֹ, וְאֵלּוּ הֵן:

פֶּסַח. מַצָּה. וּמָרוֹר:

פֶּסַח

שֶׁהָיוּ אֲבוֹתֵינוּ אוֹכְלִים, בִּזְמַן שֶׁבֵּית הַמִּקְדָּשׁ הָיָה קַיָּם, עַל שׁוּם מָה? עַל שׁוּם שֶׁפָּסַח הַקָּדוֹשׁ בָּרוּךְ הוּא, עַל בָּתֵּי אֲבוֹתֵינוּ בְּמִצְרַיִם, שֶׁנֶּאֱמַר: וַאֲמַרְתֶּם זֶבַח פֶּסַח הוּא לַיהוה, אֲשֶׁר פָּסַח עַל־ בָּתֵּי בְנֵי־יִשְׂרָאֵל בְּמִצְרַיִם, בְּנָגְפּוֹ אֶת־מִצְרַיִם וְאֶת־בָּתֵּינוּ הִצִּיל, וַיִּקֹּד הָעָם וַיִּשְׁתַּחֲווּ.

Rabban Gamliel used to say: Anyone who has not discussed these three things on Passover has not fulfilled his obligation, and they are:

Pesach, the Passover offering; Matzah, the unleavened bread; and Marror, the bitter herbs.

Pesach

Why did our fathers eat the Passover offering during the period of the Temple? It is because the Holy One, blessed be He, passed over the houses of our forefathers in Egypt, as it is said: "And you shall say: It is the Passover offering for the Lord, Who passed over the houses of the children of Israel in Egypt when He smote the Egyptians and spared our houses. And the people knelt and bowed down."

The middle matzah is lifted or pointed to while the following paragraph is recited:

מַצָּה

זוּ שֶׁאָנוּ אוֹכְלִים, עַל שׁוּם מַה? עַל שׁוּם שֶׁלֹּא הִסְפִּיק בְּצֵקָם שֶׁל
אֲבוֹתֵינוּ לְהַחֲמִיץ, עַד שֶׁנִּגְלָה עֲלֵיהֶם מֶלֶךְ מַלְכֵי הַמְּלָכִים, הַקָּדוֹשׁ בָּרוּךְ
הוּא, וּגְאָלָם, שֶׁנֶּאֱמַר: וַיֹּאפוּ אֶת־הַבָּצֵק, אֲשֶׁר הוֹצִיאוּ מִמִּצְרַיִם, עֻגֹת
מַצּוֹת, כִּי לֹא חָמֵץ: כִּי־גֹרְשׁוּ מִמִּצְרַיִם, וְלֹא יָכְלוּ לְהִתְמַהְמֵהַּ, וְגַם־צֵדָה
לֹא־עָשׂוּ לָהֶם.

The marror is lifted or pointed to while the following paragraph is recited:

זֶה שֶׁאָנוּ אוֹכְלִים עַל שׁוּם מַה? עַל שׁוּם שֶׁמֵּרְרוּ הַמִּצְרִים אֶת־חַיֵּי
אֲבוֹתֵינוּ בְּמִצְרָיִם שֶׁנֶּאֱמַר: וַיְמָרְרוּ אֶת־חַיֵּיהֶם בַּעֲבֹדָה קָשָׁה בְּחֹמֶר
וּבִלְבֵנִים וּבְכָל־עֲבֹדָה בַּשָּׂדֶה; אֵת כָּל־עֲבֹדָתָם אֲשֶׁר עָבְדוּ בָהֶם בְּפָרֶךְ.

The middle matzah is lifted or pointed to while the following paragraph is recited:

Matzah

Why do we eat this matzah? It is because the King of Kings, the Holy One, blessed be He, revealed Himself to our fathers and redeemed them before their dough had time to ferment, as it is said: "And they baked the dough which they had brought out of Egypt into unleavened cakes because it did not rise; for they were driven out of Egypt and could not delay, nor had they prepared any provision for their journey."

The marror is lifted or pointed to while the following paragraph is recited:

Marror

Why do we eat this bitter herb? It is because the Egyptians embittered the lives of our fathers in Egypt, as it is said: "And they made life bitter for them with hard labor, with clay and with bricks, and with all kinds of labor in the field; whatever work tasks they performed were backbreaking."

B'CHOL DOR VADOR CHAYAV ADAM IN EVERY GENERATION EVERYONE IS OBLIGATED.

Of all the things we are told to do on Pesach, perhaps the most difficult one is found in the words *"chayav adam lirot et atzmo k'ilu hu yatzah mimitzrayim"* – every Jew is supposed to look upon himself as if he had actually gone out of Egypt. All of the rituals – the eating of the matzah and the bitter herb, and everything else -are meant to help us see ourselves as having experienced the Egyptian bondage. We're supposed to lift ourselves up out of our suburban homes and imagine ourselves back in the hovels and huts of Egypt. As Rabbi Jack Riemer has noted, it's not easy to do that, but we've got to learn to do it, because the ability to see – to really see – beyond ourselves is the key to understanding what this holiday is all about. Indeed, our whole redemption came about because of it. Moses had the ability to see beyond himself, to see beyond his culture and to see how others see themselves. The Bible describes how Moses went out one day and saw people suffering. He was no longer a detached Egyptian prince, but he saw humans being tormented and he felt their pain; although he was a prince, he was able to put himself in the place of a slave.

And that's what the whole Pesach experience is meant to do to us. *Chayav adam lirot et atzmo k'ilu hu yatzah mimitzrayim* – it is hard, terribly hard, for any of us to see ourselves and feel ourselves as if we had gone forth out of Egypt. And yet, hard as it may be, we are supposed to perform that kind of an act of imagination if we are really to enter into the spirit of Passover.

We have to perform that kind of an act of imagination not only with those who went forth out of Egypt, but with those surrounding us as well. Unless we are able to feel with each other, unless we are able to imagine ourselves in each other's situations, we will never be able to achieve true understanding, cooperation and peace.

A rabbi tells of how he visits patients in the hospital several days a week. He tries not to miss anyone, although these days you can have a heart transplant in the morning, and your insurance company thinks you're well enough to go home for lunch. The rabbi tries to be sympathetic to the person's pain and to be understanding of the patient's complaints. Inevitably, the view is different if you're the visitor rather than the one lying in the hospital bed. But one year his mother was hospitalized and all of a sudden, he was not a rabbi anymore, he was a son. And all of a sudden, this wasn't a patient anymore, this was his mother. And all of a sudden, he wasn't so sympathetic and understanding anymore – he was angry! They had taken his mother and made her a number with a silly white gown and a band on her arm that identified her by code. And they had left her lying on a cot waiting hours for an MRI, and then informing her it was too late in the day to have it done; she had to be brought back down tomorrow. His mother was made to feel as if she was nobody! And now when he makes hospital visits, he sees what he didn't see before: staff talking about the patient in front of the patient as if he or she were already dead. The endless hours waiting nervously when a test was promised for that morning and at three in the afternoon nothing's happened. Being told, as one of his members was, that the insurance company said, time's up, time to go home. This on a Friday night, 10 o'clock at night; and when the patient said, "I have no way of getting home," they called him a cab!

Would whoever called the cab have done it if that patient had been his mother? Do any of us stop to think of what it's like to be on the other side? *Chayav adam lirot et atzmo* – it would be good if all of us could have the experience of changing roles once in a while. If only the lawyer could be a client, the rabbi a congregant, the doctor a patient, and the social worker a welfare recipient – at least for a day or two. It would make a big difference in the way we treat and judge and understand each other.

- Are you able to put yourself in the place of others?
- Are you able to put yourself in the place of your parents, feeling their worries and concerns?
- Are you able to put yourself in the place of your children, feeling their angst?
- Are you able to put yourself in the place of the homeless?
- The handicapped?
- The people of Darfur?
- Where is Darfur?

בְּכָל־דּוֹר וָדוֹר חַיָּב אָדָם לִרְאוֹת אֶת־עַצְמוֹ כְּאִלּוּ הוּא יָצָא מִמִּצְרַיִם שֶׁנֶּאֱמַר: וְהִגַּדְתָּ לְבִנְךָ בַּיּוֹם הַהוּא לֵאמֹר: בַּעֲבוּר זֶה עָשָׂה יהוה לִי בְּצֵאתִי מִמִּצְרָיִם. לֹא אֶת־אֲבוֹתֵינוּ בִּלְבָד גָּאַל הַקָּדוֹשׁ בָּרוּךְ הוּא אֶלָּא אַף אוֹתָנוּ גָּאַל עִמָּהֶם שֶׁנֶּאֱמַר: וְאוֹתָנוּ הוֹצִיא מִשָּׁם לְמַעַן הָבִיא אֹתָנוּ לָתֶת לָנוּ אֶת־הָאָרֶץ אֲשֶׁר נִשְׁבַּע לַאֲבֹתֵינוּ.

In every generation it is man's duty to regard himself as though he personally had come out of Egypt, as it is said: "And you shall tell your son on that day: This is on account of what the Lord did for me when I came out of Egypt." It was not only our fathers whom the Holy One blessed be He redeemed; we, too, were redeemed with them, as it is said: "And He took us out from there so that He might bring us to give us the land which He had sworn to our fathers."

L'FIKACH ANACHNU CHAYAVIM L'HODOT
THEREFORE IT IS OUR DUTY TO THANK.

The first words a Jew utters every day are, "*Modeh ani* – I give thanks." Expressing thanksgiving to God takes on special meaning during the festival of Pesach. In the words of Rabbi Joseph Soloveitchik, "The essence of the Seder and hence that of 'telling the story of the exodus from Egypt' is the expression of gratitude to the Almighty on the great liberation and miracles that He wrought for us in Egypt." As Maimonides puts it, "We are commanded to tell the story at the beginning of the 15th of Nisan … and we are to thank Him for all the goodness He has bestowed upon us." Expressing gratitude is very important.

Gratitude is something the people of France would do well to learn. America's war with Iraq brought with it some serious consequences, one of which was a severe setback in relations between the French and American governments, with a sentiment growing among many Americans that we should boycott all things made in France. The Internet is filled with sites ridiculing France and its leaders with lines like: "The French are always there … when they need you!" Even if one was opposed to President Bush's decision to go to war against Iraq, one must still be appalled by France's behavior. France – like every other country – had the right to disagree with America. But it's one thing for a nation to say to us: We understand what you are doing, but we cannot participate militarily. It is another when a nation says it won't support us diplomatically. It is quite another when a nation organizes opposition to us, effectively putting our forces at greater risk, giving the enemy hope, which could have stiffened their resistance in time of war. And this is exactly what France did.

According to the American Battle Monuments Commission, there are 26,255 American dead from World War I buried in four cemeteries in

France. There are 30,426 American dead from World War II buried in six cemeteries in France. That's 56,681 brave American heroes who died in their youth to liberate a country which now does so much to undermine America's efforts; a country whose Prime Minister, when told that eight East European countries were siding with America in this battle, said, "This would have been a good opportunity for them to shut up"; whose Foreign Minister, when asked by a reporter if he wanted the U.S. led forces to win the war, could not bring himself to say a simple "yes"; and a country where one-third of those polled said they hoped America would lose the war!

How can you explain it? Don't the French people and their leaders remember what we did for them? Don't they remember how we were there for them in their time of need? The answer is: yes ... and no. And to understand the answer, one must go back in time to the period of our enslavement in Egypt. How did that enslavement start? The Jews were well integrated into Egyptian society. Starting with Joseph, Jews had made important contributions to Egyptian society. What happened? Says the Torah: *"Vayakom melech chadash asher lo yoda et Yosef* – and a new king arose who did not know Joseph." Joseph – the Jew sold into slavery in Egypt, thrown into prison, interpreter of the king's dreams, who rose to the position of assistant to the king, and who ultimately saved the Egyptian economy from famine. Ask our sages: How is it possible that one generation later this king already forgot about what Joseph had done; *"V'halo ad hayom hazeh mitzrayim yodin chasido shel Yosef* - to this very day Egyptian history records what Joseph did for the Egyptian people"? How could it be that this king "did not know Joseph"?

Answer our sages: *"Asa atzmo k'ilo lo yoda* – he made himself as if he didn't know." He didn't remember Joseph because he didn't want to remember Joseph! To remember the good that someone did for you can be a heavy burden. After all, you then owe that person a debt of gratitude. And who wants to owe anybody anything? Not the Egyptians to the Jews in days of old ... and not the French to the American people in our day and age. Do the French people remember what we did for them? Sure! It's right there before their very eyes: right by the Seine River there is a large street named for President Woodrow Wilson, and a major boulevard cutting into the renowned Champs Elysees is named for President Franklin Delano Roosevelt. The famed Paris metro has a station named for Roosevelt; it is one stop before the station named for Charles DeGaulle. It is impossible for the French people to forget what we did for them during two World Wars, but they make themselves as if they don't remember. "*Asa atzmo k'ilo lo yada.*" It's much easier that way.

Another way of saying "thanks" is the phrase "much obliged." To feel gratitude is to feel a sense of obligation. To be grateful is to be burdened with a sense of indebtedness, and no one wants to feel indebted. It's one of the more unfortunate aspects of life. Often the people you do the most for are the people who turn against you. Haven't you experienced it? Now, as Americans, we have all experienced it.

We, as Jews, are constantly reminded not to fall into this trap. Moses is referred to as "*Moshe Rabbeinu*" – Moshe, our teacher. Indeed, even his name "Moshe" teaches us the importance of gratitude. What was Moshe's name? We say Moshe or Moses, but that's not really so. That name was given to him by Pharaoh's daughter as a child. To escape Egyptian persecution he was placed in a basket, floated down the river, discovered by the daughter of Pharaoh and called "Moshe," "*Ki min hamayim mishitihu* – because I drew him out of the water." But what was the name given to him at birth by his parents? It's never stated in the Bible. He is always called by this name "Moshe" given by Pharaoh's daughter. Why? So that her act of kindness would never be forgotten. Even God referred to him as "Moshe" as a debt of gratitude to Pharaoh's daughter.

• Do you express your gratitude to God? To your parents? To your children? To your wife/husband?
• Do you sometimes make yourself as if you didn't know the good someone did for you? Why?
• Do you feel that you are taken for granted by your friends and family?

The cup is lifted, and the matzot are covered. The following paragraphs are said:

לְפִיכָךְ אֲנַחְנוּ חַיָּבִים לְהוֹדוֹת, לְהַלֵּל, לְשַׁבֵּחַ, לְפָאֵר, לְרוֹמֵם, לְהַדֵּר,
לְבָרֵךְ, לְעַלֵּה וּלְקַלֵּס, לְמִי שֶׁעָשָׂה לַאֲבוֹתֵינוּ וְלָנוּ אֶת־כָּל־הַנִּסִּים הָאֵלּוּ.
הוֹצִיאָנוּ מֵעַבְדוּת לְחֵרוּת, מִיָּגוֹן לְשִׂמְחָה, וּמֵאֵבֶל לְיוֹם טוֹב, וּמֵאֲפֵלָה
לְאוֹרָה, וּמִשִּׁעְבּוּד לִגְאֻלָּה. וְנֹאמַר לְפָנָיו שִׁירָה חֲדָשָׁה. הַלְלוּיָהּ:

הַלְלוּיָהּ. הַלְלוּ עַבְדֵי יהוה, הַלְלוּ אֶת־שֵׁם יהוה. יְהִי שֵׁם יהוה מְבֹרָךְ
מֵעַתָּה וְעַד־עוֹלָם. מִמִּזְרַח־שֶׁמֶשׁ עַד־מְבוֹאוֹ, מְהֻלָּל שֵׁם יהוה. רָם
עַל־כָּל־גּוֹיִם יהוה, עַל־הַשָּׁמַיִם כְּבוֹדוֹ.

מִי כַּיהוה אֱלֹהֵינוּ, הַמַּגְבִּיהִי לָשָׁבֶת. הַמַּשְׁפִּילִי לִרְאוֹת, בַּשָּׁמַיִם וּבָאָרֶץ.
מְקִימִי מֵעָפָר דָּל, מֵאַשְׁפֹּת יָרִים אֶבְיוֹן. לְהוֹשִׁיבִי עִם־נְדִיבִים, עִם
נְדִיבֵי עַמּוֹ. מוֹשִׁיבִי עֲקֶרֶת הַבַּיִת, אֵם־הַבָּנִים שְׂמֵחָה. הַלְלוּיָהּ.

The cup is lifted, and the matzot are covered. The following paragraphs are said:

Therefore it is our duty to thank and praise, pay tribute and glorify, exalt and honor, bless, raise high, and acclaim the One Who performed all these miracles for our fathers and for us. He took us out of slavery into freedom, out of grief into joy, out of mourning into a festival, and out of darkness into a great light, and out of slavery into redemption. And we will recite a new song before Him! Halleluyah! (Praise the Lord!)

Praise the Lord! Praise, you servants of the Lord, praise the name of the Lord. Blessed be the name of the Lord from this time forth and forever. From the rising of the sun to its setting, the Lord's name is to be praised. High above all nations is the Lord; above the heavens is His glory.

Who is like the Lord our God, Who, though enthroned on high, looks down upon heaven and earth? He raises the poor man out of the dust and lifts the needy one out of the trash heap, to seat him with nobles, with the nobles of His people. He turns the barren wife into a happy mother of children. Halleluyah! (Praise the Lord!)

בְּצֵאת יִשְׂרָאֵל מִמִּצְרָיִם, בֵּית יַעֲקֹב מֵעַם לֹעֵז. הָיְתָה יְהוּדָה לְקָדְשׁוֹ, יִשְׂרָאֵל מַמְשְׁלוֹתָיו. הַיָּם רָאָה וַיָּנֹס, הַיַּרְדֵּן יִסֹּב לְאָחוֹר. הֶהָרִים רָקְדוּ כְאֵילִים, גְּבָעוֹת כִּבְנֵי־צֹאן. מַה־לְּךָ הַיָּם כִּי תָנוּס, הַיַּרְדֵּן תִּסֹּב לְאָחוֹר. הֶהָרִים תִּרְקְדוּ כְאֵילִים, גְּבָעוֹת כִּבְנֵי־צֹאן. מִלִּפְנֵי אָדוֹן חוּלִי אָרֶץ מִלִּפְנֵי אֱלוֹהַּ יַעֲקֹב. הַהֹפְכִי הַצּוּר אֲגַם־מָיִם, חַלָּמִישׁ לְמַעְיְנוֹ־מָיִם.

The cup is lifted, and the matzot are covered during the recitation of the following blessing:

בָּרוּךְ אַתָּה יְהוָה, אֱלֹהֵינוּ מֶלֶךְ הָעוֹלָם, אֲשֶׁר גְּאָלָנוּ וְגָאַל אֶת־אֲבוֹתֵינוּ מִמִּצְרַיִם, וְהִגִּיעָנוּ הַלַּיְלָה הַזֶּה, לֶאֱכָל בּוֹ מַצָּה וּמָרוֹר. כֵּן, יְהוָה אֱלֹהֵינוּ וֵאלֹהֵי אֲבוֹתֵינוּ, יַגִּיעֵנוּ לְמוֹעֲדִים וְלִרְגָלִים אֲחֵרִים, הַבָּאִים לִקְרָאתֵנוּ לְשָׁלוֹם. שְׂמֵחִים בְּבִנְיַן עִירֶךָ, וְשָׂשִׂים בַּעֲבוֹדָתֶךָ, וְנֹאכַל שָׁם מִן הַזְּבָחִים וּמִן הַפְּסָחִים (במוצאי שבת אומרים: מִן הַפְּסָחִים וּמִן הַזְּבָחִים), אֲשֶׁר יַגִּיעַ דָּמָם, עַל קִיר מִזְבַּחֲךָ לְרָצוֹן, וְנוֹדֶה לְךָ שִׁיר חָדָשׁ עַל גְּאֻלָּתֵנוּ, וְעַל פְּדוּת נַפְשֵׁנוּ. בָּרוּךְ אַתָּה יְהוָה, גָּאַל יִשְׂרָאֵל:

When Israel went out of Egypt, Jacob's household from a people of strange language, Judah became God's sanctuary, Israel His kingdom. The sea saw it and fled; the Jordan turned backward. The mountains skipped like rams, and the hills like lambs. Why is it, sea, that you flee? Why, O Jordan, do you turn backward? You mountains, why do you skip like rams? You hills, why do you leap like lambs? O Earth, tremble at the Lord's presence, at the presence of the God of Jacob, who turns the rock into a pond of water, the flint into a flowing fountain of waters.

The cup is lifted, and the matzot are covered during the recitation of the following blessing:

God You are the source of blessing, our God, King of the universe, Who has redeemed us and our fathers from Egypt, and enabled us to reach this night that we may eat matzah and marror. So, Lord our God and God of our fathers, enable us to reach also the forthcoming holidays and festivals which will come to us in peace, rejoicing in the rebuilding of Zion, Your city, and joyful at Your service. There, we shall eat of the offerings and Passover sacrifices (On Saturday night: of the Passover sacrifices and offerings) whose blood will be acceptably placed upon Your altar. We shall sing a new hymn of praise to You for our redemption and for our spiritual liberation. God, You are the source of blessing, Who has redeemed Israel.

(הִנְנִי מוּכָן וּמְזוּמָּן לְקַיֵּם מִצְוַת כּוֹס שְׁנִיָּה מֵאַרְבַּע כּוֹסוֹת לְשֵׁם יִחוּד
קוּדְשָׁא בְּרִיךְ הוּא וּשְׁכִינְתֵּיהּ עַל־יְדֵי הַהוּא טָמִיר וְנֶעְלָם בְּשֵׁם כָּל־יִשְׂרָאֵל.)

בָּרוּךְ אַתָּה יהוה, אֱלֹהֵינוּ מֶלֶךְ הָעוֹלָם, בּוֹרֵא פְּרִי הַגָּפֶן:

The hands are washed, and the following blessing is recited:

בָּרוּךְ אַתָּה יהוה אֱלֹהֵינוּ מֶלֶךְ הָעוֹלָם, אֲשֶׁר קִדְּשָׁנוּ בְּמִצְוֹתָיו, וְצִוָּנוּ עַל
נְטִילַת יָדָיִם:

God, You are the source of blessing, our God, King of the universe, Who creates the fruit of the vine.

Wash Hands for the Meal

The hands are washed, and the following blessing is recited:

God, You are the source of blessing, our God, King of the universe, Who has sanctified us with His commandments, and commanded us concerning the washing of the hands.

MOTZI, MATZAH
THE BLESSING OVER THE MATZAH

It has been said that all Jewish holidays can be succinctly summarized in the words, "They tried to kill us … we won … let's eat!" Finally, the moment we've all waited for … FOOD! We wash our hands, recite the appropriate blessings, and eat the matzah. But watch out! Keep that matzah away from water!

Some will find this hard to believe, but there are many Jews who, on Pesach, do not eat any cooked product that requires matzah coming in contact with water. That is called "*gebrokt*," which really means "dipped" or "broken" matzah, although the more appropriate designation is "*matzah sheruah* – soaked matzah."

That's quite a tradition – followed by all Chasidim and others – prohibiting the eating of any matzah that soaks in a liquid. That cuts out matzah balls and matzah brei and matzah latkes. That means you don't use any matzah meal, cake meal or matzah farfel in your cooking. What is the basis for this prohibition? Flour that comes in contact with water and is allowed to sit for 18 minutes, causing it to rise and become leavened, turns into chometz. All of our matzah products, therefore, are made of flour and water that baked for less than 18 minutes. So what's with *gebrokt*? The Mishneh Berurah, the most respected Jewish code of law of the 20th century, explains, "There are people who are meticulous about how they act, who are stringent with themselves and do not soak or cook matzah on Pesach. The reason is that they are afraid that a little flour may have remained in the matzah on the inside, which was not kneaded properly, and it would become leavened through the soaking." The concern is that some part of the matzah may not have been fully baked and is still primarily flour, and when this flour comes in contact with a liquid, after 18 minutes it will turn into chometz.

But the Mishneh Berurah goes on to quote another Halachic authority, the Shaarei Teshuvah, who writes that "from the standpoint of basic

Halacha one need not be concerned about this fear since we do not presume forbidden circumstances without any foundation," and the Shaarei Teshuvah adds: *"D'achuzka issura lo machzekinin* – don't go creating prohibitions that are not there."

The Shaarei Teshuvah is telling us that this is an unnecessary concern, that the concern may have been legitimate in our East European days when the matzah that was baked was very thick. Then there could have been pockets in the matzah where the flour had not been fully baked. But in our day, when matzah is made thin, there is no need for this stringency.

There are two important lessons that the Jewish community could learn from this lesson of *gebrokt*. First, a mindset has developed, most certainly within the Orthodox community, that the stricter, the better. More stringent means you are more religious. And *gebrokt* teaches us that it ain't necessarily so. Stricter is not necessarily better ... more stringent does not necessarily equal more pious.

But even those who are strict with *gebrokt* will tell you that those people who follow this prohibition, who will not eat any matzah product that is soaked in liquid, have a remarkable custom on the eighth day of Pesach. They specifically make it their business to eat matzah that is soaked in liquid on the eighth day of Pesach! They do this as a way of telling Jews who eat *gebrokt* all Pesach long: our custom is no reflection on you. It doesn't mean that we think that you're eating chometz. We don't think less of you for not taking on this stringency, and to prove it, on the last day of Pesach we're going to eat *gebrokt* just like you do!

All of us as Jews can learn from *"gebrokt"* all year round. It is telling us that no Jew should take a "holier than thou" attitude toward his fellow Jews. It is telling us that each of us should follow our own way, without casting aspersions on what other Jews do.

- Do you know people who are "too" pious for their own good?
- Do you know any "frummies?"
- Is that a term of endearment?
- Do you think there are "good" Jews and "bad" Jews?
- What makes them good or bad?
- Which one are you?

MATZAH

Whereas we are Biblically commanded not to eat chometz during the entire festival of Pesach, the commandment to eat matzah pertains only to the first two nights. The matzah serves a twofold purpose, symbolizing both our affliction and our journey to freedom. It is amazing how an item made simply of wheat (although several other grains are permitted) and water has undergone so many changes over the centuries. Originally, the matzah was soft; now it is hard. Once it was very thick; now it is rather thin. What used to be made by hand is now primarily made by machine. The handmade is oval; the machine made is square. And of course, what was once just matzah is now whole wheat matzah, egg matzah, onion matzah, salted matzah and chocolate covered matzah! Not to mention kosher-for-Pesach pizza crust – perhaps to commemorate the exodus of the Jews from Sicily!

But as many changes as the matzah has undergone, for observant Jews, on the first two nights of Pesach and for many during the entire festival, only "Shmurah" - "watched" matzah is used. Shmurah matzah is matzah whose wheat was watched and supervised from the time it was cut until after it was baked. The matzah is usually made in a small bakery used just for Pesach where the" watched" flour is mixed with pure spring water and flattened with a wooden rolling pin – all within 18 minutes.

Eating Shmurah matzah is important, but in the eyes of Rabbi Israel Salanter it wasn't enough. Rabbi Salanter was the moving force behind the "Mussar" movement in the 19th century, which stressed the importance of ethics combined with ritual. Rabbi Salanter was the supervisor of a Shmurah matzah bakery. The story is told that one year he refused to give a kosher certification to the bakery. When asked why by the owner, he said, "Because you exploit and underpay your workers." To Rabbi Salanter's way of thinking, being kosher was not simply a matter of the ingredients in a product, but of the manner of behavior as well.

A modern manifestation of this way of thinking recently came to light in Israel where there is a new rabbinic certification sponsored by the Tzohar Rabbinical Association, comprising Religious Zionist rabbis. Their certifying organization is called "*Bemaagalei Tzedek*" – "ways of justice." Their certification is different from all the others because it goes way beyond the food. According to *The Jerusalem Post*, "In order to get their certificate a proprietor must be able to check off every item on a checklist drawn up by the organization and agree to allow weekly inspections by a member of the *Bemaagalei Tzedek* Task Force. Items on the list include: wheelchair accessibility, a guarantee of minimum wage for workers, not employing minors or foreign workers and paying for workers' transportation to and from work."

This is a beautiful concept. It provides a broader understanding of what the word "kosher" means. It goes way beyond food. Kosher means "fit" and "proper." And this new rabbinic certification understands that "fit and proper" refers not just to an animal, but also to a human being. "Fit and proper" must be the way we serve not only our God, but our fellow man.

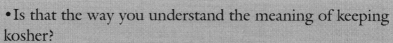

?
- Is that the way you understand the meaning of keeping kosher?
- Do you believe that understanding our rituals and practicing them can make you into a more ethical human being?
- Is there a purpose in keeping kosher inside your home but not outside?
- Is that hypocritical?
- Or, is "something better than nothing?"

מוֹצִיא. מַצָּה

The following two blessings are recited over the matzah. The first is the regular blessing for bread, which praises God for the matzah as food. The second is the special blessing only recited on Seder night, which praises God for the clear obligation to eat matzah tonight. The second blessing should be made with the intention that it also applies to Korech and the Afikoman.

The head of the household raises all the matzot on the Seder Plate and says the following blessings:

בָּרוּךְ אַתָּה יהוה, אֱלֹהֵינוּ מֶלֶךְ הָעוֹלָם, הַמּוֹצִיא לֶחֶם מִן הָאָרֶץ:

Those who use three matzot put down the bottom one at this point.

בָּרוּךְ אַתָּה יהוה, אֱלֹהֵינוּ מֶלֶךְ הָעוֹלָם, אֲשֶׁר קִדְּשָׁנוּ בְּמִצְוֹתָיו וְצִוָּנוּ עַל אֲכִילַת מַצָּה:

Blessings over the Matzah

The following two blessings are recited over the matzah. The first is the regular blessing for bread, which praises God for the matzah as food. The second is the special blessing only recited on Seder night, which praises God for the clear obligation to eat matzah tonight. The second blessing should be made with the intention that it also applies to Korech and the Afikoman.

The head of the household raises all the matzot on the Seder Plate and says the following blessings:

God, You are the source of blessing, our God, King of the universe, Who brings forth bread from the earth.

Those who use three matzot put down the bottom one at this point.

God, You are the source of blessing, our God, King of the universe, Who has sanctified us with His commandments, and commanded us concerning the eating of matzah.

Each person is required to eat an amount of matzah equal to the volume of half an egg, kebeitza, (2.5-3.3 oz.) which is approximately one quarter of a machine made matzah or one fifth of a hand made matzah. Since it is usually impossible to provide this amount from the top two matzot on the Seder Plate, other matzot should be available to obtain the required portion. However, each person should receive a piece from the top two matzot. Also, during the Seder only shmurah matzah (matzah that has been very carefully watched during the process of making it) should be used. The matzot should be eaten while reclining on the left side.

Maror
The Bitter Herb

The eating of the bitter herb is a central part of the Pesach observance, reminding us how the Egyptians embittered the lives of our ancestors.

According to the Mishnah, several types of plants are considered maror, including romaine lettuce, endive or escarole, and horseradish. According to our sages, romaine lettuce is the ideal for maror. And yet, so many use horseradish. The reality is, it was only in the 14th and 15th centuries that the sages in Eastern Europe identified horseradish as being one of the acceptable plants. East European Jews were forced to use horseradish for the maror by necessity; they didn't have Trader Joe's or Whole Foods where they could purchase romaine lettuce. It was only horseradish that was available at that time of the year. In our day, more and more are turning to romaine lettuce. Romaine lettuce is considered the ideal for fulfilling the obligation of eating maror because, in the words of the Jerusalem Talmud, "In the same manner that the lettuce is at first sweet and then later becomes bitter, so is the situation of our ancestors in Egypt." At first the Jews were welcomed with open arms when they settled in the land of Egypt. Gradually, the Egyptians turned against them, enslaving them and making their lives bitter.

What happened to our ancestors in Egypt has been true, for the most part, of all of our ancestors in all the countries in which they settled. At first, they were welcomed, but eventually they were moved into ghettos, suffered pogroms and were expelled.

The American experience has been a unique one for the Jews, reversing the experience of our ancestors in Egypt and other lands. In America, at first we were not welcomed. It was in September of 1654 when a small boat with 23 Jews who had been expelled from Brazil sailed into New Amsterdam, the present day New York. They were greeted by a well-known figure in American history, Peter Stuyvesant. How were the Jews welcomed? With Peter Stuyvesant refusing to let them in, calling the Jews "deceitful," "very repugnant," and "hateful enemies and blasphemers of the name of Christ." Imagine … they didn't want Jews in New York! And now, 350 years later, New York has the largest Jewish population of any city in the world.

How do you explain the fact that while Jews represent less than 3% of the population, 10% of the U.S. Senate is Jewish, as is the majority of the Presidents at Ivy League universities, and faculties and student bodies at elite colleges and universities are typically 30% - 40% Jewish? An article in *The Forward* newspaper related a story of someone sitting in a café in London on February 28, 2001 reading the *International Herald Tribune*. He couldn't get over the fact that, when he turned to the editorial page, five of the six columns were written by Jews: Richard Cohen, Stephen Rosenfeld, Robert Caplan, Ellen Goodman and Thomas Friedman. The sixth column was written by a South Korean by the name of Professor Han Sung-Joo. Five Jews … and a Joo! It's true, with so many Jewish names, it makes some of our enemies think that we control the world. But for the most part, the reality is that in America Jews form a high percentage among writers, nationally syndicated journalists, intellectuals, publishers and Hollywood executives. According to an Anti-Defamation League survey, 32% of the people living in Europe believe that Jews have too much influence over the financial markets. Here in America the person most in control of the economy is the chairman of the Federal Reserve Board. Alan Greenspan, a Jew, held that position for 18 years. When he retired he was replaced by Benjamin S. Bernanke … Ben Bernanke, whose father was a kosher butcher and whose middle initial stands for "Shalom!" We've made it in America!

- Why IS America different?
- Is it?
- To what do you attribute Jewish successes?
- Will they continue in the next generations?

מָרוֹר

The head of the household gives a kezayit (1.1-1.25 oz.) size of marror dipped in charoset to each participant. The following blessing is recited with the intention that it also apply to the marror on the korech sandwich. It should be eaten without reclining.

בָּרוּךְ אַתָּה יהוה אֱלֹהֵינוּ מֶלֶךְ הָעוֹלָם, אֲשֶׁר קִדְּשָׁנוּ בְּמִצְוֹתָיו וְצִוָּנוּ עַל אֲכִילַת מָרוֹר:

Bitter Herbs Dipped in Charoset

The head of the household gives a kezayit (1.1-1.25 oz.) size of marror dipped in charoset to each participant. The following blessing is recited with the intention that it also apply to the marror on the korech sandwich. It should be eaten without reclining.

God, You are the source of blessing, our God, King of the universe, Who has sanctified us with His commandments, and commanded us concerning the eating of bitter herbs.

KORECH
THE SANDWICH

Biblically there were three food items that had to be eaten on Pesach: matzah, maror and the Pascal lamb. Our sages questioned whether these three foods were to be eaten separately or together. So after their being eaten separately, Hillel made it a tradition in the time of the Temple to eat the three together. What did he eat? He took a piece of matzah, put a piece of Pesach – lamb – on top of it and on top of that put a piece of maror. As children, this moment at the Seder filled us with pride, as we learned that it was Hillel – not the Lord of Sandwich – who created the first sandwich. But the reality is, it wasn't a sandwich in its original form. What was it? Matzah topped with some lamb and some horseradish? It was an hors d'oeuvre! Hillel was not the creator of the sandwich. Hillel was the creator of the hors d'oeuvre! So what happened to that hors d'oeuvre? Rabbi Lawrence Hoffman, Professor of Liturgy at the Hebrew Union College – Jewish Institute of Religion, has written a most thought provoking article on this subject. Professor Hoffman points out that after the Temple was destroyed we no longer had the Pascal sacrifice. What did we have? We still had the matzah, we still had the maror, but we needed something as a replacement for the Pascal sacrifice. That second piece of matzah is not there because we wanted to make a sandwich – it was never intended to be a sandwich! That second piece of matzah is there as a replacement for the korban Pesach, the Paschal lamb. But why was matzah chosen? Because we needed something that symbolized redemption and salvation as the Pascal lamb had done, and we needed something to represent hope for the future redemption after the destruction of the Temple. Matzah was a perfect symbol because bread in general has salvational symbolism.

The Midrash pictures the Garden of Eden replete with bread trees as large as the cedars of Lebanon, about which our rabbis tell us, "*Sh'hu atid lehotsi lechem min ha'arets* – that in the future God will bring forth bread from the earth." In other words, the blissful state of the Garden of Eden will someday be replicated once more, and bread will come from the ground. Bread, therefore, symbolized future deliverance, a perfect replacement to be used for the missing Pesach sacrifice. At the Seder we couldn't use bread so we used the other wheat product – matzah.

This is why we have that second piece of matzah as part of the korech and this is also why Jesus – in his spiritual Sermon on the Mount – uses the expression "give us this day our daily bread." Why in a speech about salvation and the future in heaven does Jesus speak about "daily bread?" Because he was knowledgeable and learned in the Jewish tradition, and he understood that bread represented something more than just food to eat; bread and the future way that God will give it to us symbolized salvation. Jesus and Paul were using their Jewish roots in identifying bread as a symbol of deliverance.

- Did you know that in our tradition bread was a symbol of deliverance?
- Did you know that Jesus was knowledgeable and learned in the Jewish tradition?
- How can you explain why Jesus knew more about Judaism than many Jews living today?
- What are you going to do about that?

כּוֹרֵךְ

זֵכֶר לְמִקְדָּשׁ כְּהִלֵּל: כֵּן עָשָׂה הִלֵּל בִּזְמַן שֶׁבֵּית הַמִּקְדָּשׁ הָיָה קַיָּם. הָיָה כּוֹרֵךְ
פֶּסַח מַצָּה וּמָרוֹר וְאוֹכֵל בְּיַחַד. לְקַיֵּם מַה שֶׁנֶּאֱמַר: עַל־מַצּוֹת וּמְרוֹרִים יֹאכְלֻהוּ:

שֻׁלְחָן עוֹרֵךְ

This part of the Seder constitutes the meal. While the meal is eaten, any extraneous conversation should be avoided. One should also remember that the afikoman should be eaten while there is still some appetite for it. Therefore, one should not fill himself beyond the point that he will have to force the afikoman down, for to do so would negate the mitzvah.

צָפוּן

From the afikoman, one should eat the volume of a kezayit, before midnight while reclining and nothing may be eaten or drunk after eating the afikoman, except for the last two cups of wine.

Marror and Matzah Sandwich

The bottom, thus far unbroken matzah is now taken. From it, with the addition of other matzot, each person receives half an egg volume of matzah with an equal portion of marror (dipped into charoset which is shaken off). The following paragraph is recited and the "sandwich" is eaten while reclining.

To remind us of the Temple we do as Hillel did in Temple times: He combined the Pesach lamb, matzah and marror in a sandwich and ate them together, to fulfill what is said in the Torah: "They shall eat it (the pesach lamb) with unleavened bread (matzah) and bitter herbs."

Serve the Meal

This part of the Seder constitutes the meal.

Partaking of the Afikoman

From the afikoman, and if necessary, from additional matzot, one should eat the volume of a kezayit, which is equivalent to the volume of half an egg or, as mentioned previously, one quarter of a machine made matzah, or one fifth of a hand made matzah. It should be eaten before midnight while reclining and nothing may be eaten or drunk after eating the afikoman, except for the last two cups of wine.

80

BIRKAT HAMAZON
GRACE AFTER MEALS

The Birkat Hamazon is recited at the conclusion of every meal. In so doing we fulfill the Biblical commandment, "And you shall eat and be satisfied and you should bless the Lord your God for the goodly land which He gave you." (Deuteronomy 8:10) The Birkat Hamazon comprises four blessings, three of which come from the Biblical period.

The first blessing thanks God for giving us sustenance and is attributed to Moses when the mannah descended in the desert.

The second blessing, which thanks God "for the land", is attributed to Joshua when the Jews entered the land of Israel.

The third blessing, which expresses the hope for the rebuilding of Jerusalem, is attributed to King David who established Jerusalem as the capital of Israel, and to his son Solomon who built the Temple.

The fourth blessing, referring to God as "*hatov v'hamativ* – good, who does good," is a later addition related to an event that took place in the 2nd century C.E. Thousands of Jews were massacred at Betar. The Romans left their dead bodies exposed, but miraculously, the bodies did not decay. In recognition of that miracle, and in gratitude for the opportunity to bury them, our sages added this fourth blessing.

It seems rather strange that a blessing would be added which commemorates not a joyous moment in the history of the Jews, but one associated with so much pain and sorrow. Rabbi Joseph Soloveitchik explained that our sages added this blessing because, in seeing that the bodies had not decayed, they saw God's protective hand. From the time of the destruction of the Temple until that time, the Jews had experienced one calamity after another, and wondered: Does God care? Is God there? Now, with the miracle at Betar, they knew that God was there and that God cared.

It's not always easy seeing God's hand during dark times. Some are able to do it. After the tragedy of 9/11 when many asked: Where was God? the response of some was: He was with the millions who were saved. Yittah Halberstam, in her book, *Small Miracles for the Jewish Heart*, tells the story of a small synagogue near the twin towers where many Jews who worked in the towers would gather every morning for Shacharit services. For some reason, on the morning of September 11th, only nine men showed up. And so they waited and waited for a tenth. After a long wait, which meant they would be late for work, someone whom they had never seen before entered the room, saying he came because he had to say kaddish. They invited him to lead the services and he proved to be a very slow *davener* which made things even later ... so late, that while they were *davening* the first plane crashed into the twin towers and all those present had the same feeling: it could have been us, were it not for our having waited for the tenth man and for his having prayed so slowly. They turned to thank this mystery man who had saved their lives, but the story concludes by telling us, "When they turned around to embrace him, the man was gone, his identity forever a mystery."

This story is but one of many that explains God's presence on September 11th as being made manifest in the thousands and thousands of people who survived the collapse of the twin towers. That's where God was! But for many, that lets God off the hook too easily. Elie Weisel, in writing of God, so properly proclaimed: "To thank Him for Jerusalem and not question him for Treblinka is hypocrisy." To say that God was with those who were saved on September 11th, but not with those who were killed on September 11th, leaves more questions than answers. To say that He was in the room with those ten people who prayed in the minyan while the twin towers were hit, but was not in the rooms in the minyanim that took place earlier that day is difficult to believe.

So what do you believe? We all see and experience so much pain, grief, loss and disappointment in our personal lives and in our collective lives. And ultimately the choice is ours – to believe or not to believe. But who is better off? On April 11, 2002, thirteen Israeli soldiers were killed in the battle in the Jenin refugee camp. Two days later there was an article in *The Jerusalem Post* about the funerals that had taken place for these fallen soldiers. And these are the exact words in which two of them were described. First there was the story of Gadalyah Malik, all of 20 years old. His father, Simcha Malik, was abroad working for the Jewish Agency when he heard the news of his son's death. He returned for the funeral, but standing in the cemetery ready to say goodbye to his son, he said: "It's not clear that we are parting one from the other. What does that mean? Who understands the way of God? Yesterday when his mother called with the news, she said, 'God gave us a gift and now we have returned it.' Thank you, God, for the gift we received," his father said.

Then came the funeral of Sgt. Major Avner Yaskov, with these words: "Speaking yesterday at the funeral of her husband at the military cemetery in Beersheva, Penina Yaskov asked God: Why did you take him from me? I don't believe in you anymore and I am no longer going to pray to you."

Two reactions of families to similar circumstances: the loss of a loved one taken all too soon. And both reactions are understandable. We can either cry out and curse God or we can bless and thank God.

- What do you do?
- What should you do?
- Believe, or not believe? That is the question.

The third cup of wine is poured and the Birkat HaMazon (the Grace after Meals) is recited. Upon the completion of Birkat HaMazon, the blessing over the wine is recited and the third cup of wine is drunk while reclining on the left side. Preferably, one should drink the entire cup. At the least, most of the cup should be drunk.

שִׁיר הַמַּעֲלוֹת בְּשׁוּב יהוה אֶת שִׁיבַת צִיּוֹן הָיִינוּ כְּחֹלְמִים: אָז יִמָּלֵא שְׂחוֹק פִּינוּ וּלְשׁוֹנֵנוּ רִנָּה. אָז יֹאמְרוּ בַגּוֹיִם הִגְדִּיל יהוה לַעֲשׂוֹת עִם אֵלֶּה: הִגְדִּיל יהוה לַעֲשׂוֹת עִמָּנוּ הָיִינוּ שְׂמֵחִים: שׁוּבָה יהוה אֶת שְׁבִיתֵנוּ כַּאֲפִיקִים בַּנֶּגֶב: הַזֹּרְעִים בְּדִמְעָה בְּרִנָּה יִקְצֹרוּ: הָלוֹךְ יֵלֵךְ וּבָכֹה נֹשֵׂא מֶשֶׁךְ הַזָּרַע בֹּא יָבֹא בְרִנָּה נֹשֵׂא אֲלֻמֹּתָיו:

Some add the following:

(תְּהִלַּת יהוה יְדַבֶּר פִּי, וִיבָרֵךְ כָּל בָּשָׂר שֵׁם קָדְשׁוֹ לְעוֹלָם וָעֶד. וַאֲנַחְנוּ נְבָרֵךְ יָהּ, מֵעַתָּה וְעַד עוֹלָם, הַלְלוּיָהּ. הוֹדוּ לַיהוה כִּי טוֹב, כִּי לְעוֹלָם חַסְדּוֹ. מִי יְמַלֵּל גְּבוּרוֹת יהוה, יַשְׁמִיעַ כָּל תְּהִלָּתוֹ.)

Grace after Meals

The third cup of wine is poured and the Birkat HaMazon (the Grace after Meals) is recited. Upon the completion of Birkat HaMazon, the blessing over the wine is recited and the third cup of wine is drunk while reclining on the left side. Preferably, one should drink the entire cup. At the least, most of the cup should be drunk.

Psalm 126

A Song of Ascents. When the Lord brought the exiles back to Zion, we were like dreamers. Then our mouth was filled with laughter, and our tongue with glad song. Then it will be said among the nations: "The Lord has done great things for them." The Lord had done great things for us, and we rejoiced. Restore our captives, O Lord, like streams in the Negev. Those who sow in tears shall reap in joy. Though the farmer bears the measure of seed to the field in sadness, he shall come home with joy, bearing his sheaves.

Some add the following:

(May my mouth declare the praise of the Lord and may all flesh bless His holy name forever. And we will bless the Lord from this time and forever, Halleluyah (Praise the Lord)! Give thanks to the Lord for He is good, for His kindness endures forever. Who can express the mighty acts of the Lord, or can declare all His praise?!)

The following (until "בְּרוּך אתה") is added when three or more males over the age of Bar Mitzvah (over the age of thirteen) are present. The phrase "אלהינו" in parentheses is added if a minyan (ten men above the age of Bar Mitzvah) is present.*

הַמזַמֵּן: רַבּוֹתַי נְבָרֵךְ!

הַמסוּבִּין: יְהִי שֵׁם יהוה מְבֹרָךְ מֵעַתָּה וְעַד עוֹלָם.

הַמזַמֵּן: יְהִי שֵׁם יהוה מְבֹרָךְ מֵעַתָּה וְעַד עוֹלָם.
בִּרְשׁוּת מָרָנָן וְרַבָּנָן וְרַבּוֹתַי, נְבָרֵךְ (אֱלֹהֵינוּ) שֶׁאָכַלְנוּ מִשֶּׁלּוֹ.

הַמסוּבִּין: בָּרוּךְ (אֱלֹהֵינוּ) שֶׁאָכַלְנוּ מִשֶּׁלּוֹ וּבְטוּבוֹ חָיִינוּ.

הַמזַמֵּן: בָּרוּךְ (אֱלֹהֵינוּ) שֶׁאָכַלְנוּ מִשֶּׁלּוֹ וּבְטוּבוֹ חָיִינוּ.

כּוֹלָם: בָּרוּךְ הוּא וּבָרוּךְ שְׁמוֹ:

The following (until "Blessed be He...") is added when three or more males over the age of Bar Mitzvah (over the age of thirteen) are present. The phrase "our God" in parentheses is added if a minyan (ten men above the age of Bar Mitzvah) is present.

Leader:

Let us say grace.

Guests respond, then leader continues:

Let us now bless the name of the Lord from this time forth and forever.

Leader:

Let us now bless the name of the Lord from this time forth and forever. With your permission, let us now bless He (our God) of Whose food We have eaten.

Guests respond, then leader repeats:

Blessed be He (our God) of Whose food we have eaten and through Whose goodness we live.

All:

Blessed be He and blessed be His name

בָּרוּךְ אַתָּה יהוה, אֱלֹהֵינוּ מֶלֶךְ הָעוֹלָם, הַזָּן אֶת הָעוֹלָם כֻּלּוֹ בְּטוּבוֹ בְּחֵן בְּחֶסֶד וּבְרַחֲמִים. הוּא נוֹתֵן לֶחֶם לְכָל בָּשָׂר כִּי לְעוֹלָם חַסְדּוֹ. וּבְטוּבוֹ הַגָּדוֹל תָּמִיד לֹא חָסַר לָנוּ, וְאַל יֶחְסַר לָנוּ מָזוֹן לְעוֹלָם וָעֶד. בַּעֲבוּר שְׁמוֹ הַגָּדוֹל, כִּי הוּא אֵל זָן וּמְפַרְנֵס לַכֹּל וּמֵטִיב לַכֹּל, וּמֵכִין מָזוֹן לְכָל בְּרִיּוֹתָיו אֲשֶׁר בָּרָא. בָּרוּךְ אַתָּה יהוה, הַזָּן אֶת הַכֹּל:

נוֹדֶה לְךָ יהוה אֱלֹהֵינוּ עַל שֶׁהִנְחַלְתָּ לַאֲבוֹתֵינוּ, אֶרֶץ חֶמְדָּה טוֹבָה וּרְחָבָה, וְעַל שֶׁהוֹצֵאתָנוּ יהוה אֱלֹהֵינוּ מֵאֶרֶץ מִצְרַיִם, וּפְדִיתָנוּ, מִבֵּית עֲבָדִים, וְעַל בְּרִיתְךָ שֶׁחָתַמְתָּ בִּבְשָׂרֵנוּ, וְעַל תּוֹרָתְךָ שֶׁלִּמַּדְתָּנוּ, וְעַל חֻקֶּיךָ שֶׁהוֹדַעְתָּנוּ וְעַל חַיִּים חֵן וָחֶסֶד שֶׁחוֹנַנְתָּנוּ, וְעַל אֲכִילַת מָזוֹן שָׁאַתָּה זָן וּמְפַרְנֵס אוֹתָנוּ תָּמִיד, בְּכָל יוֹם וּבְכָל עֵת וּבְכָל שָׁעָה:

וְעַל הַכֹּל יהוה אֱלֹהֵינוּ אֲנַחְנוּ מוֹדִים לָךְ, וּמְבָרְכִים אוֹתָךְ, יִתְבָּרַךְ שִׁמְךָ בְּפִי כָּל חַי תָּמִיד לְעוֹלָם וָעֶד. כַּכָּתוּב, וְאָכַלְתָּ וְשָׂבָעְתָּ, וּבֵרַכְתָּ אֶת יהוה אֱלֹהֶיךָ עַל הָאָרֶץ הַטֹּבָה אֲשֶׁר נָתַן לָךְ. בָּרוּךְ אַתָּה יהוה, עַל הָאָרֶץ וְעַל הַמָּזוֹן:

God, You are the source of blessing, our God, King of the universe, Who nourishes the whole world with goodness, with grace, with kindness and with mercy. He gives bread to all creatures, for His kindness endures forever. And through this great goodness we have never been in want; and may we never be in want of sustenance. For His great name's sake, for He is the God Who sustains all, and does good to all, and provides food for all the creatures which He has created. God, You are the source of blessing, Who sustains all.

We thank You, Lord our God, for having given a beautiful, good, and spacious land to our fathers as a heritage; and for having taken us out, Lord our God, from the land of Egypt and for redeeming us from the house of slavery; and for Your covenant which You have sealed in our flesh; and for Your Torah, which You have taught us; and for Your statutes, which You have made known to us; and for the life, grace and kindness which You have bestowed on us; and for the food with which You sustain us always, on every day and at all times.

And for everything, Lord our God, we thank You and bless You. May Your name be constantly blessed by all living things forever and ever, as it is written: "And when you have eaten and are satisfied, and you shall bless the Lord your God for the good land He has given you." God, You are the source of blessing, for the land and for the food.

רַחֵם (נָא) יהוה אֱלֹהֵינוּ, עַל יִשְׂרָאֵל עַמֶּךָ, וְעַל יְרוּשָׁלַיִם עִירֶךָ, וְעַל צִיּוֹן מִשְׁכַּן כְּבוֹדֶךָ, וְעַל מַלְכוּת בֵּית דָּוִד מְשִׁיחֶךָ, וְעַל הַבַּיִת הַגָּדוֹל וְהַקָּדוֹשׁ שֶׁנִּקְרָא שִׁמְךָ עָלָיו.

אֱלֹהֵינוּ, אָבִינוּ, רְעֵנוּ, זוּנֵנוּ, פַּרְנְסֵנוּ, וְכַלְכְּלֵנוּ, וְהַרְוִיחֵנוּ, וְהַרְוַח לָנוּ יהוה אֱלֹהֵינוּ מְהֵרָה מִכָּל צָרוֹתֵינוּ, וְנָא, אַל תַּצְרִיכֵנוּ יהוה אֱלֹהֵינוּ, לֹא לִידֵי מַתְּנַת בָּשָׂר וָדָם, וְלֹא לִידֵי הַלְוָאָתָם. כִּי אִם לְיָדְךָ הַמְּלֵאָה, הַפְּתוּחָה, הַקְּדוֹשָׁה וְהָרְחָבָה, שֶׁלֹּא נֵבוֹשׁ וְלֹא נִכָּלֵם לְעוֹלָם וָעֶד:

On Shabbat add the paragraph in parentheses:

(רְצֵה וְהַחֲלִיצֵנוּ יהוה אֱלֹהֵינוּ בְּמִצְוֹתֶיךָ וּבְמִצְוַת יוֹם הַשְּׁבִיעִי הַשַּׁבָּת הַגָּדוֹל וְהַקָּדוֹשׁ הַזֶּה. כִּי יוֹם זֶה גָּדוֹל וְקָדוֹשׁ הוּא לְפָנֶיךָ, לִשְׁבָּת בּוֹ וְלָנוּחַ בּוֹ בְּאַהֲבָה כְּמִצְוַת רְצוֹנֶךָ וּבִרְצוֹנְךָ הָנִיחַ לָנוּ יהוה אֱלֹהֵינוּ, שֶׁלֹּא תְהֵא צָרָה וְיָגוֹן וַאֲנָחָה בְּיוֹם מְנוּחָתֵנוּ. וְהַרְאֵנוּ יהוה אֱלֹהֵינוּ בְּנֶחָמַת צִיּוֹן עִירֶךָ, וּבְבִנְיַן יְרוּשָׁלַיִם עִיר קָדְשֶׁךָ, כִּי אַתָּה הוּא בַּעַל הַיְשׁוּעוֹת וּבַעַל הַנֶּחָמוֹת:)

Have mercy, Lord our God, on Israel Your nation, and on Jerusalem Your city, and on Zion, the abode of Your glory, and on the kingdom of the house of David, Your anointed one, and on the great and holy Temple that bears Your name.

Our God, our Father, tend and feed us, support us and sustain us and relieve us. And grant us speedily, Lord, our God, relief. And make us not rely, O Lord, our God, on the gifts and loans of men, but rather, on Your full, open, holy, and generous hand, that we may never be put to shame and disgrace.

On Shabbat add the paragraph in parentheses:

(Favor us and strengthen us, Lord, our God, with Your commandments, and with the commandment concerning the seventh day, this great and holy Sabbath. For this day is great and holy before You to abstain from work and rest on it in love according to Your will. And in Your will, Lord, our God, grant us rest so that there be no trouble, sorrow or grief on our day of rest. And let us, Lord, our God, see Zion, Your city, comforted, and Jerusalem, Your holy city, rebuilt, for You are Master of salvation and Master of consolation.)

אֱלֹהֵינוּ וֵאלֹהֵי אֲבוֹתֵינוּ, יַעֲלֶה וְיָבֹא וְיַגִּיעַ, וְיֵרָאֶה, וְיֵרָצֶה, וְיִשָּׁמַע, וְיִפָּקֵד, וְיִזָּכֵר זִכְרוֹנֵנוּ וּפִקְדוֹנֵנוּ, וְזִכְרוֹן אֲבוֹתֵינוּ, וְזִכְרוֹן מָשִׁיחַ בֶּן דָּוִד עַבְדֶּךָ, וְזִכְרוֹן יְרוּשָׁלַיִם עִיר קָדְשֶׁךָ, וְזִכְרוֹן כָּל עַמְּךָ בֵּית יִשְׂרָאֵל לְפָנֶיךָ, לִפְלֵיטָה לְטוֹבָה לְחֵן וּלְחֶסֶד וּלְרַחֲמִים, לְחַיִּים וּלְשָׁלוֹם בְּיוֹם חַג הַמַּצּוֹת הַזֶּה. זָכְרֵנוּ יְהוָה אֱלֹהֵינוּ בּוֹ לְטוֹבָה. וּפָקְדֵנוּ בּוֹ לִבְרָכָה. וְהוֹשִׁיעֵנוּ בוֹ לְחַיִּים, וּבִדְבַר יְשׁוּעָה וְרַחֲמִים, חוּס וְחָנֵּנוּ, וְרַחֵם עָלֵינוּ וְהוֹשִׁיעֵנוּ, כִּי אֵלֶיךָ עֵינֵינוּ, כִּי אֵל מֶלֶךְ חַנּוּן וְרַחוּם אָתָּה:

וּבְנֵה יְרוּשָׁלַיִם עִיר הַקֹּדֶשׁ בִּמְהֵרָה בְיָמֵינוּ. בָּרוּךְ אַתָּה יְהוָה, בּוֹנֵה (בְּרַחֲמָיו) יְרוּשָׁלָיִם. אָמֵן.

בָּרוּךְ אַתָּה יְהוָה אֱלֹהֵינוּ מֶלֶךְ הָעוֹלָם, הָאֵל אָבִינוּ, מַלְכֵּנוּ, אַדִּירֵנוּ בּוֹרְאֵנוּ, גּוֹאֲלֵנוּ, יוֹצְרֵנוּ, קְדוֹשֵׁנוּ קְדוֹשׁ יַעֲקֹב, רוֹעֵנוּ רוֹעֵה יִשְׂרָאֵל. הַמֶּלֶךְ הַטּוֹב, וְהַמֵּטִיב לַכֹּל, שֶׁבְּכָל יוֹם וָיוֹם הוּא הֵטִיב, הוּא מֵטִיב, הוּא יֵיטִיב לָנוּ. הוּא גְמָלָנוּ, הוּא גוֹמְלֵנוּ, הוּא יִגְמְלֵנוּ לָעַד לְחֵן וּלְחֶסֶד וּלְרַחֲמִים וּלְרֶוַח הַצָּלָה וְהַצְלָחָה בְּרָכָה וִישׁוּעָה, נֶחָמָה, פַּרְנָסָה, וְכַלְכָּלָה, וְרַחֲמִים, וְחַיִּים וְשָׁלוֹם, וְכָל טוֹב, וּמִכָּל טוֹב לְעוֹלָם אַל יְחַסְּרֵנוּ:

Our God, and God of our fathers, may the remembrance of us, and our account, and the remembrance of our fathers, and of the anointed son of David Your servant, and of Jerusalem, Your holy city, and of all Your people the house of Israel, ascend, and come, and reach, and appear, and be accepted, and be heard, and be counted, and be remembered before You for deliverance and good, for grace, for kindness and for mercy, for life and for peace on this day of the Festival of Matzot. Remember us this day, Lord our God, for goodness; and consider us for blessing; and save us for life. And with a word of salvation and mercy, spare us and favor us; and have pity on us and save us, for to You are our eyes turned, for You are a gracious and merciful God and King.

And rebuild Jerusalem, the holy city, speedily in our days. God, You are the source of blessing, (merciful) Builder of Jerusalem. Amen.

God, You are the source of blessing, Our God, King of the universe, God You are our Father, our King our Sovereign, our Creator, our Redeemer, our Maker, our Holy One of Jacob, our Shepherd, the good King Who does good to all; He, at all times has done good, is doing good, and will do good. He bestowed, He bestows, and He will bestow grace, kindness, and mercy, relief and deliverance, success, blessing, salvation, and comfort, and sustenance, and support, and mercy, life and peace and all goodness. And may He never deprive us of any good thing.

הָרַחֲמָן, הוּא יִמְלוֹךְ עָלֵינוּ לְעוֹלָם וָעֶד.

הָרַחֲמָן, הוּא יִתְבָּרַךְ בַּשָּׁמַיִם וּבָאָרֶץ.

הָרַחֲמָן, הוּא יִשְׁתַּבַּח לְדוֹר דּוֹרִים, וְיִתְפָּאַר בָּנוּ לָעַד וּלְנֵצַח נְצָחִים,
וְיִתְהַדַּר בָּנוּ לָעַד וּלְעוֹלְמֵי עוֹלָמִים.

הָרַחֲמָן, הוּא יְפַרְנְסֵנוּ בְּכָבוֹד.

הָרַחֲמָן, הוּא יִשְׁבּוֹר עֻלֵנוּ מֵעַל צַוָּארֵנוּ וְהוּא יוֹלִיכֵנוּ קוֹמְמִיּוּת לְאַרְצֵנוּ.

הָרַחֲמָן, הוּא יִשְׁלַח לָנוּ בְּרָכָה מְרֻבָּה בַּבַּיִת הַזֶּה, וְעַל שֻׁלְחָן זֶה
שֶׁאָכַלְנוּ עָלָיו.

הָרַחֲמָן, הוּא יִשְׁלַח לָנוּ אֶת אֵלִיָּהוּ הַנָּבִיא זָכוּר לַטּוֹב, וִיבַשֶּׂר לָנוּ
בְּשׂוֹרוֹת טוֹבוֹת יְשׁוּעוֹת וְנֶחָמוֹת.

At parents' table, add:

הָרַחֲמָן, הוּא יְבָרֵךְ אֶת אָבִי מוֹרִי בַּעַל הַבַּיִת הַזֶּה, וְאֶת אִמִּי מוֹרָתִי
בַּעֲלַת הַבַּיִת הַזֶּה, אוֹתָם וְאֶת בֵּיתָם וְאֶת זַרְעָם וְאֶת כָּל אֲשֶׁר לָהֶם,

---

May the Merciful One reign over us forever and ever.

May the Merciful One be blessed in heaven and on earth.

May the Merciful One be praised for all generations; and may He be glorified through us forever and ever; and may He be extolled through us for all eternity.

May the Merciful One grant us an honorable livelihood.

May the Merciful One break the yoke from our neck; and may He lead us upstanding into our land.

May the Merciful One send ample blessing into this house and upon this table at which we have eaten.

May the Merciful One send us Elijah the Prophet of blessed memory who will bring us good tidings of consolation and comfort.

At parents' table, add:

May the Merciful One bless my revered father the master of this house, and my revered mother the mistress of this house, them, their house, their children, and all that belongs to them.

At one's own table, add:

הָרַחֲמָן, הוּא יְבָרֵךְ אוֹתִי וְאֶת אִשְׁתִּי/בַּעֲלִי וְאֶת זַרְעִי וְאֶת כָּל אֲשֶׁר לִי,

When a guest, add:

הָרַחֲמָן, הוּא יְבָרֵךְ אֶת בַּעַל הַבַּיִת הַזֶּה וְאֶת אִשְׁתּוֹ בַּעֲלַת הַבַּיִת הַזֶּה,
אוֹתָם וְאֶת בֵּיתָם וְאֶת זַרְעָם וְאֶת כָּל אֲשֶׁר לָהֶם,

All Continue:

אוֹתָנוּ וְאֶת כָּל אֲשֶׁר לָנוּ, כְּמוֹ שֶׁנִּתְבָּרְכוּ אֲבוֹתֵינוּ, אַבְרָהָם יִצְחָק וְיַעֲקֹב:
בַּכֹּל, מִכֹּל, כֹּל. כֵּן יְבָרֵךְ אוֹתָנוּ כֻּלָּנוּ יַחַד. בִּבְרָכָה שְׁלֵמָה, וְנֹאמַר אָמֵן:

בַּמָּרוֹם יְלַמְּדוּ עֲלֵיהֶם וְעָלֵינוּ זְכוּת, שֶׁתְּהֵא לְמִשְׁמֶרֶת שָׁלוֹם,
וְנִשָּׂא בְרָכָה מֵאֵת יהוה וּצְדָקָה מֵאֱלֹהֵי יִשְׁעֵנוּ, וְנִמְצָא חֵן וְשֵׂכֶל
טוֹב בְּעֵינֵי אֱלֹהִים וְאָדָם:

On Shabbat add the sentence in parentheses:

(הָרַחֲמָן, הוּא יַנְחִילֵנוּ יוֹם שֶׁכֻּלּוֹ שַׁבָּת וּמְנוּחָה לְחַיֵּי הָעוֹלָמִים.)

At one's own table, add:

May the Merciful One bless myself, my wife/my husband, and children and all that belongs to me.

When a guest, add:

May the Merciful One bless the master of this house, and his wife the mistress of this house, them, their house, their children, and all that belongs to them.

All Continue:

[May He bless] us all together and all our possessions just as He blessed our forefathers Avraham, Yitzhak, and Yaakov, with everything. May He bless us all together with a perfect blessing, and let us say, Amen.

May they in heaven find merits with us so that we may enjoy a lasting peace. And may we receive blessings from the Lord, and charity from the God of our salvation, and may we find favor and good sense in the eyes of God and men.

On Shabbat add the sentence in parentheses:

(May the Merciful One cause us to inherit the day which will be all Sabbath and rest in the eternal life.)

הָרַחֲמָן, הוּא יַנְחִילֵנוּ יוֹם שֶׁכֻּלּוֹ טוֹב.

הָרַחֲמָן, הוּא יְזַכֵּנוּ לִימוֹת הַמָּשִׁיחַ וּלְחַיֵּי הָעוֹלָם הַבָּא. מַגְדִּיל יְשׁוּעוֹת
מַלְכּוֹ, וְעֹשֶׂה חֶסֶד לִמְשִׁיחוֹ לְדָוִד וּלְזַרְעוֹ עַד עוֹלָם: עֹשֶׂה שָׁלוֹם בִּמְרוֹמָיו,
הוּא יַעֲשֶׂה שָׁלוֹם עָלֵינוּ וְעַל כָּל יִשְׂרָאֵל, וְאִמְרוּ אָמֵן:

יְראוּ אֶת יהוה קְדֹשָׁיו, כִּי אֵין מַחְסוֹר לִירֵאָיו: כְּפִירִים רָשׁוּ וְרָעֵבוּ,
וְדֹרְשֵׁי יהוה לֹא יַחְסְרוּ כָל טוֹב: הוֹדוּ לַיהוה כִּי טוֹב, כִּי לְעוֹלָם
חַסְדּוֹ: פּוֹתֵחַ אֶת יָדֶךָ, וּמַשְׂבִּיעַ לְכָל חַי רָצוֹן: בָּרוּךְ הַגֶּבֶר אֲשֶׁר יִבְטַח
בַּיהוה, וְהָיָה יהוה מִבְטַחוֹ: נַעַר הָיִיתִי גַם זָקַנְתִּי וְלֹא רָאִיתִי צַדִּיק
נֶעֱזָב, וְזַרְעוֹ מְבַקֶּשׁ לָחֶם: יהוה עֹז לְעַמּוֹ יִתֵּן, יהוה יְבָרֵךְ אֶת עַמּוֹ בַשָּׁלוֹם:

(הִנְנִי מוּכָן וּמְזֻמָּן לְקַיֵּם מִצְוַת כּוֹס שְׁלִישִׁית מֵאַרְבַּע כּוֹסוֹת לְשֵׁם יִחוּד
קוּדְשָׁא בְּרִיךְ הוּא וּשְׁכִינְתֵּיהּ עַל יְדֵי הַהוּא טָמִיר וְנֶעְלָם בְּשֵׁם כָּל יִשְׂרָאֵל.)

בָּרוּךְ אַתָּה יהוה, אֱלֹהֵינוּ מֶלֶךְ הָעוֹלָם, בּוֹרֵא פְּרִי הַגָּפֶן:

May the Merciful One cause us to inherit the day of total goodness.

May the Merciful One make us worthy to see the days of the Mashiach and the life of the world to come. He is the tower of salvation of His chosen king and does kindness to His anointed one, to David and to his descendants forever. He Who creates peace in His heavenly heights, may He grant peace for us and for all Israel; and say Amen.

Revere the Lord, you, His holy ones, for those who revere Him suffer no want. Young lions may be famishing and starving, but those who seek the Lord shall not lack any good thing. Give thanks to the Lord, for He is good; For His kindness endures forever. You open Your hand and satisfy the desire of every living thing. Blessed is the man who trusts in the Lord, and whose trust is in the Lord. I have been young and now I am old, but never have I seen a righteous man forsaken, nor his children wanting bread. The Lord will give strength to His people; the Lord will bless His people with peace.

God, You are the source of blessing, our God, King of the universe, Who creates the fruit of the vine.

SHEFOCH CHAMATCHA
POUR FORTH THY WRATH

This passage makes many Jews uncomfortable. Indeed, in some Haggadahs, the paragraph is completely removed. That is an injustice … an injustice to the history of the Jewish people.

This prayer, or more so, this statement, which is made up of several Biblical verses, was added to the Haggadah in the Middle Ages when the Jews were suffering terrible persecutions by the Christians. Because of its proximity to Easter, the Pesach season was always a very difficult period for Jews; it was a time of remembrance of the death of Jesus which was blamed upon the Jews and which was constantly exploited by the Christian clergy to fan anti-Jewish hatred. Passover was the season for reviving the blood libel that accused Jews of killing Gentile babies and using their blood to prepare the matzah and wine for the Seder. On Seder night the Gentiles often staged vicious pogroms against their Jewish neighbors, making it necessary to open the door and look out into the street, lest, God-forbid, a dead baby had been placed near the house to provide the mob with a pretext to ravage and kill. In England and France and Spain, in Poland and Russia and Ukraine, there were horrible pogroms – Jews were driven from their homes, and many massacred – all on the night of Pesach. And what could the Jews do about this? They could do nothing. All they could do was cry out, and that's exactly what they did with the Shefoch Chamatcha prayer. It was inserted to be recited at the time when we pour the cup for Elijah with the hope that soon he would come and usher in the Messianic era.

Jews are uncomfortable with the phrases found in Shefoch Chamatcha because they seem to underscore an ancient stereotype of the difference between Judaism and Christianity. Christians have long claimed that they believe in love and that Jews believe in vengeance. Their God is merciful; the Jewish God is harsh and demanding. Jews are primitive; they are civilized. Jewish spiritual growth has been stunted; Christianity long ago surpassed Judaism.

In a sermon written by Rabbi Dr. Norman Lamm nearly a half-century ago, he discussed this subject and pointed out, "The record does not show any genocide on the part of the Jewish people: we talk strongly against Amalek but it was not we who utterly destroyed them. The chronicles of our people do not reveal that Jews ever built concentration camps. It was not the genius of Jews that invented gas chambers. Our prophets did not incite mobs to pogroms against non-Jews. On the contrary, they saw visions of universal peace and righteousness. They reminded us that other peoples are also God's children. We never went on crusades; we have no history of inquisitions. In fact, we passed into Jewish law the requirement that where we become dominant in a community, it is incumbent upon us to care for the Gentile sick, poor and hungry no less than our own." The fact of the matter is, Judaism is the one that practiced love. Christianity is the one which practiced vengeance. All this is part of the historical record of Jewish/Christian relations.

There is one verse in the Shefoch Chamatcha that says: "For they have consumed Jacob and laid waste his habitation." In Talmudic literature Jacob always represented the Jewish people, and his brother Esau – also known as Edom – represented Rome – the Christian world. The conflict between Jacob and Esau when they were young represented to our sages the eternal conflict between the Jews and Christians. What happened with Jacob and Esau? After years of separation and threats by Esau to kill Jacob, they are finally reunited. And the Torah tells us: "And Esau ran toward Jacob and embraced him and he fell on his neck and kissed him and cried." The rabbis in the Midrash have contradictory opinions over this reconciliation and just how sincere Esau was.

It is important to keep in mind an insight into the story of Jacob and Esau that was given by the head of the famed Volozhin Yeshiva, who wrote in his book *Ha-amek Davar*: "Both wept, implying that Jacob's love was aroused toward Esau. And so it is in all ages. Whenever the seed of Esau is prompted by sincere motives to acknowledge and respect the offspring of Israel, then we, too, are moved to acknowledge Esau, for he is our brother." What this Torah giant is saying is that when the

Christian world extends a hand of friendship to the Jews, we dare not turn our backs but must respond in kind.

We have come a long way in our day. It started with Pope John XXIII, who after centuries of Church anti-Semitism, turned to the Jewish people and said, "I am Joseph, your brother." Those words, spoken in the Bible, began the reconciliation of the children of Jacob. Whether Pope John's words can bring about reconciliation between the children of Isaac remains to be seen. But for the first time in 2000 years there is some hope ... some hope of genuine brotherhood.

It is interesting to note that according to the Christians, Jacob represents Christianity and Esau represents the Jews! After all, Esau was the older brother, just as the Jews are the older brother. It was Jerome, an early Christian saint, who taught, "Isaac conveys a figure of God the father; Rebecca of the Holy Spirit; Esau of the first people and the devil; Jacob of the Church or of Christ." This underscores the fact that Jews and Christians see things differently, and always will! Jews are not going to convince Christians that Jacob represents the Jews and Esau represents the Christians, any more than Christians can convince Jews of the reverse. Genuine brotherhood and interfaith relations are going to have to come about not by blurring differences, but by respecting differences. Christians and Jews are always going to see things differently ... from the Messiah to Mel Gibson ... and all points in between.

• Do you think Christians have truly changed their attitude toward the Jewish people?
• Do you consider the embrace extended to Jews by evangelical Christians a blessing or a curse?

The fourth cup of wine is poured. According to most customs, the cup of Eliyahu is filled at this point and then the door is opened. Then the following paragraph is recited:.

שְׁפֹךְ חֲמָתְךָ אֶל־הַגּוֹיִם, אֲשֶׁר לֹא יְדָעוּךָ וְעַל־מַמְלָכוֹת אֲשֶׁר בְּשִׁמְךָ לֹא קָרָאוּ: כִּי אָכַל אֶת־יַעֲקֹב. וְאֶת־נָוֵהוּ הֵשַׁמּוּ: שְׁפָךְ־עֲלֵיהֶם זַעְמֶךָ, וַחֲרוֹן אַפְּךָ יַשִּׂיגֵם: תִּרְדֹּף בְּאַף וְתַשְׁמִידֵם, מִתַּחַת שְׁמֵי יהוה:

The fourth cup of wine is poured. According to most customs, the cup of Eliyahu is filled at this point and then the door is opened. Then, the following paragraph is recited:

Pour out Your wrath on the nations that do not know You and on the kingdoms that do not call Your name. For they have devoured Yaakov and laid waste his dwelling place. Pour out Your rage on them and let Your fierce anger overtake them. Pursue them with anger and destroy them from beneath God's heavens.

HALLEL
PSALMS OF PRAISE

The Hallel, comprising six psalms of praise to God, is recited on festive days in the Jewish calendar. But at no time does it take on more meaning than during the festival of Pesach. In Temple times, the Hallel was recited as an accompaniment to the slaughtering of the Pascal Lamb on the afternoon preceding Pesach, and recited once again at the Seder itself. To this day, some have the custom of reciting it an additional time at the evening service ushering in the festival of Pesach.

Surprisingly, while a full version of the Hallel is recited at the Seder and on the first days of Pesach, an abbreviated version of the Hallel - referred to as the "half Hallel" - is recited on the other six days of this festival. The Talmud and Midrash explain that the last days of Pesach focus not on the exodus from Egypt, but on the miraculous crossing of the Red Sea. According to tradition, when the Egyptians were drowned, the angels wanted to sing a hymn of praise to the Almighty, but God said, "How can you rejoice and sing my praises when the works of my hands are drowning in the sea?" We Jews do not rejoice when our enemies suffer. When reciting the Ten Plagues at the Seder we remove a drop of wine from our cups at the mention of each plague. Our cups can't be full when our enemies are in pain. Indeed, we are taught in The Book of Proverbs: "*Binfol oyvecha al tismach* – when your enemy falls do not rejoice."

In our time, during the Intifada at the beginning of the 21st century, Israel exhibited sensitivity to its enemies that no other country would have shown. Of course, for some, whatever Israel did to defend itself against terrorism was no good. Blockade their cities – no good! Shoot at their snipers – no good! Withhold their taxes – no good! Target their suicide bombers – no good! Seize their property – no good! Every time Israel responded to a Palestinian attack, Western governments accused Israel's response of being "reprehensible," "excessive," "disproportionate," "provocative," "an escalation," etc. etc. All this overlooked the real facts, the facts that while America was bombing whole city streets in Iraq, Israeli soldiers were sent into homes of terror suspects, putting their lives on the line in order to reduce the possibility of civilian casualties. As Michael Oren, the award winning author of *Six Days of War*, points out, when U.S. forces believed that Saddam Hussein was hiding in a certain neighborhood in Baghdad, U.S. planes flattened the neighborhood, but when the IDF learned that the entire leadership of Hamas was in a single building in Gaza, it chose a bomb too small to eliminate them for fear of harming nearby civilians.

Mr. Oren goes on to write:

> Israel today faces challenges every bit as existential as those Ben-Gurion confronted in 1948. Terrorists still try to blow themselves up in public places within Israel, and vast forces, many armed with long-range missiles and unconventional weapons, assemble around it. As evidenced recently by Iranian President Mahmoud Ahmadinejad's call for Israel to be 'wiped off the map,' many of the world's 1.3 billion Muslims would not weep over the disappearance of the Jewish state, nor would they be too selective with respect to the manner in which that elimination would be implemented. Many Western Europeans, meanwhile, are indifferent and even hostile to Israel's fate. And even in America--in its universities in particular--Israel is increasingly vilified, delegitimized, and branded an anachronism at best, and a fascist regime at worst. Yet, in spite of the immense forces arrayed against it, Israel has not only stood up to the test of power. Far more than that, it has presented to the world a model of balance between the requirements of justice and morality and the requisites of power. The IDF is generally regarded as one of the strongest and most sophisticated armies in the world, yet it does not use even a fraction of its potential strength against the people who, if they held such power, would hesitate not a moment to direct

it at Israel's destruction. Israel does not evict a people that threatens its existence--and the last century is rife with such expulsions, especially in the West--but rather offers that people an opportunity to live with it side by side, even offering large parts of its own historical and spiritual homeland. Israel's soldiers go into battle armed not only with guns and grenades but with pocket-size, laminated cards containing the IDF code of ethics, which reminds them that it is their solemn duty to make every effort to avoid causing civilian casualties and to use their weapons solely for the purposes of self- and national defense. Israelis fight, asking themselves at every stage whether in fact they are doing the right thing, the moral thing, the Jewish thing.

Azure Magazine, Winter 5766

What is "the Jewish thing?" Perhaps it was best described by Claude Haberman in a 2001 article in *The New York Times*. It was written at a time during the Intifada when the Israeli city of Gilo was under constant sniper barrage from the Arab village of Beth Jalla. Haberman described how the Israelis went into Beth Jalla, occupied it for 48 hours, and then withdrew. He told of how during those 48 hours, Jewish soldiers occupied a certain house and took over the top floors so that they could see and shoot at snipers from there. They pushed the people who lived in the house into a single room and kept them there under armed guard. "It was an awful experience. We weren't able to move around in our own home," the people who lived in the house complained to the reporter after the Israelis left.

So far, that's not much of a story. This is what soldiers do in every struggle. When your town gets shot at often enough, you go in and try to find the snipers and get rid of them. And, if in the process, you have to occupy somebody's house in order to do the job – then that's what you do.

The news in the story was in the last sentence. Clyde Haberman says that he went into the house after the Israelis left to see how much damage they had done. He found that, before the soldiers withdrew from the house and from Beth Jalla, they apologized. They left a note for the family. They put it into the paws of a teddy bear they found in a child's room. And this is what the note said, "We are truly sorry for the mess we made."

- Are you proud of Israel's behavior in combating terrorism?
- Are you ashamed?
- Do you have a better idea?
- How should they get out of this mess?

הַלֵּל

תהלים קטו: א-יא

לֹא לָנוּ יְהוָה לֹא לָנוּ כִּי לְשִׁמְךָ תֵּן כָּבוֹד, עַל חַסְדְּךָ עַל אֲמִתֶּךָ. לָמָּה
יֹאמְרוּ הַגּוֹיִם, אַיֵּה נָא אֱלֹהֵיהֶם. וֵאלֹהֵינוּ בַשָּׁמָיִם כֹּל אֲשֶׁר חָפֵץ
עָשָׂה. עֲצַבֵּיהֶם כֶּסֶף וְזָהָב, מַעֲשֵׂה יְדֵי אָדָם. פֶּה לָהֶם וְלֹא יְדַבֵּרוּ,
עֵינַיִם לָהֶם וְלֹא יִרְאוּ. אָזְנַיִם לָהֶם וְלֹא יִשְׁמָעוּ, אַף לָהֶם וְלֹא יְרִיחוּן.
יְדֵיהֶם וְלֹא יְמִישׁוּן, רַגְלֵיהֶם וְלֹא יְהַלֵּכוּ, לֹא יֶהְגּוּ בִּגְרוֹנָם. כְּמוֹהֶם יִהְיוּ
עֹשֵׂיהֶם, כֹּל אֲשֶׁר בֹּטֵחַ בָּהֶם: יִשְׂרָאֵל בְּטַח בַּיהוָה, עֶזְרָם וּמָגִנָּם הוּא.
בֵּית אַהֲרֹן בִּטְחוּ בַיהוָה, עֶזְרָם וּמָגִנָּם הוּא. יִרְאֵי יְהוָה בִּטְחוּ בַיהוָה,
עֶזְרָם וּמָגִנָּם הוּא:

תהלים קטו:יב – יח

יְהוָה זְכָרָנוּ יְבָרֵךְ, יְבָרֵךְ אֶת בֵּית יִשְׂרָאֵל, יְבָרֵךְ אֶת בֵּית אַהֲרֹן. יְבָרֵךְ
יִרְאֵי יְהוָה, הַקְּטַנִּים עִם הַגְּדֹלִים. יֹסֵף יְהוָה עֲלֵיכֶם, עֲלֵיכֶם וְעַל בְּנֵיכֶם.

Hallel

Psalm 115:1-11

Not for our sake, O Lord, not for our sake, but for Your name's sake, give glory, for Your kindness and Your truth. Why should the nations say: "Where is their God?" But God is in the heavens. He does whatever He desires! Their idols are silver and gold, the work of human hands. They have a mouth, but they cannot speak; they have eyes, but they cannot see; they have ears, but they cannot hear; they have a nose, but they cannot smell; they have hands, but they cannot feel; they have feet, but they cannot walk; nor can they utter a sound with their throat. Those who make them shall become like them, whoever trusts in them. O Israel, trust in the Lord! He is their help and their shield. O house of Aaron, trust in the Lord! He is their help and their shield. You, who revere the Lord, trust in the Lord! He is their help and their shield.

Psalm 115:12-18

The Lord Who has remembered us will bless; He will bless the house of Israel; He will bless the house of Aaron; He will bless those who revere the Lord, the small with the great. May the Lord increase you; you and your children.

בְּרוּכִים אַתֶּם לַיהוה, עֹשֵׂה שָׁמַיִם וָאָרֶץ. הַשָּׁמַיִם שָׁמַיִם לַיהוה,
וְהָאָרֶץ נָתַן לִבְנֵי אָדָם. לֹא הַמֵּתִים יְהַלְלוּ יָהּ, וְלֹא כָּל יֹרְדֵי דוּמָה.
וַאֲנַחְנוּ נְבָרֵךְ יָהּ, מֵעַתָּה וְעַד עוֹלָם, הַלְלוּיָהּ:

תהלים קטז:א-יא

אָהַבְתִּי כִּי יִשְׁמַע יהוה, אֶת קוֹלִי תַּחֲנוּנָי. כִּי הִטָּה אָזְנוֹ לִי וּבְיָמַי אֶקְרָא:
אֲפָפוּנִי חֶבְלֵי מָוֶת, וּמְצָרֵי שְׁאוֹל מְצָאוּנִי צָרָה וְיָגוֹן אֶמְצָא. וּבְשֵׁם יהוה
אֶקְרָא, אָנָּה יהוה מַלְּטָה נַפְשִׁי. חַנּוּן יהוה וְצַדִּיק, וֵאלֹהֵינוּ מְרַחֵם. שֹׁמֵר
פְּתָאִים יהוה דַּלּוֹתִי וְלִי יְהוֹשִׁיעַ. שׁוּבִי נַפְשִׁי לִמְנוּחָיְכִי, כִּי יהוה גָּמַל
עָלָיְכִי. כִּי חִלַּצְתָּ נַפְשִׁי מִמָּוֶת אֶת עֵינִי מִן דִּמְעָה, אֶת רַגְלִי מִדֶּחִי.
אֶתְהַלֵּךְ לִפְנֵי יהוה, בְּאַרְצוֹת הַחַיִּים. הֶאֱמַנְתִּי כִּי אֲדַבֵּר, אֲנִי עָנִיתִי
מְאֹד. אֲנִי אָמַרְתִּי בְחָפְזִי כָּל הָאָדָם כֹּזֵב.

You are blessed by the Lord, Who made the heaven and earth. The heaven is the Lord's heaven, but He has given the earth to mankind. The dead cannot praise the Lord, nor can any who go down into silence. But we will bless the Lord from this time forth and forever. Halleluyah (Praise the Lord)!

Psalm 116:1-11

I love that the Lord hears my voice and my supplications. Because He has inclined His ear to me, I will call upon Him as long as I live. The cords of death encircled me; the pains of the grave have overtaken me; I found trouble and sorrow. Then, I called upon the name of the Lord: "O Lord, save my life!" Gracious is the Lord, and righteous and our God is merciful. The Lord protects the simple; I was brought low and He saved me. Return to your rest, O my soul, for the Lord has been kind to you. You have delivered my soul from death, my eyes from tears and my feet from stumbling. I shall walk before the Lord in the lands of the living. I kept faith even when I said: "I am greatly afflicted." (I kept faith even when) I said in haste: "All men are deceitful."

מָה אָשִׁיב לַיהוה, כָּל תַּגְמוּלוֹהִי עָלָי. כּוֹס יְשׁוּעוֹת אֶשָּׂא, וּבְשֵׁם יהוה
אֶקְרָא. נְדָרַי לַיהוה אֲשַׁלֵּם, נֶגְדָה נָּא לְכָל עַמּוֹ. יָקָר בְּעֵינֵי יהוה הַמָּוְתָה
לַחֲסִידָיו. אָנָּה יהוה כִּי אֲנִי עַבְדֶּךָ אֲנִי עַבְדְּךָ, בֶּן אֲמָתֶךָ פִּתַּחְתָּ לְמוֹסֵרָי.
לְךָ אֶזְבַּח זֶבַח תּוֹדָה וּבְשֵׁם יהוה אֶקְרָא. נְדָרַי לַיהוה אֲשַׁלֵּם נֶגְדָה נָּא
לְכָל עַמּוֹ. בְּחַצְרוֹת בֵּית יהוה בְּתוֹכֵכִי יְרוּשָׁלָיִם הַלְלוּיָהּ!

הַלְלוּ אֶת יהוה, כָּל גּוֹיִם, שַׁבְּחוּהוּ כָּל הָאֻמִּים. כִּי גָבַר עָלֵינוּחַסְדּוֹ,
וֶאֱמֶת יהוה לְעוֹלָם הַלְלוּיָהּ:

כִּי לְעוֹלָם חַסְדּוֹ:	הוֹדוּ לַיהוה כִּי טוֹב,
כִּי לְעוֹלָם חַסְדּוֹ:	יֹאמַר נָא יִשְׂרָאֵל,
כִּי לְעוֹלָם חַסְדּוֹ:	יֹאמְרוּ נָא בֵית אַהֲרֹן,
כִּי לְעוֹלָם חַסְדּוֹ:	יֹאמְרוּ נָא יִרְאֵי יהוה,

Psalm 116:12-19

How can I repay the Lord for all His kind acts toward me? I will raise the cup of salvations, and call upon the name of the Lord. My vows to the Lord I will pay in the presence of all His people. Precious in the sight of the Lord is the death of His pious followers. Please, O Lord, for I am Your servant; I am Your servant, the son of Your handmaid; You have loosened my bonds. To You, I sacrifice a thanksgiving offering, and call upon the name of the Lord. My vows to the Lord, I will pay in the presence of all His people, in the courts of the Lord's house, in the midst of Jerusalem. Halleluyah (Praise the Lord)!

Psalm 117

O praise to the Lord, all you nations; praise Him, all you peoples! For His kindness overwhelms us, and the truth of the Lord is forever, Halleluyah (Praise the lord)!

Psalm 118:1-29

Give thanks to the Lord, for He is good; For His kindness endures forever.

Let Israel say: For His kindness endures forever.

Let the house of Aaron say: For His kindness endures forever.

Let those who revere the Lord say: For His kindness endures forever.

מִן הַמֵּצַר קָרָאתִי יָּה, עָנָנִי בַמֶּרְחָב יָּה. יהוה לִי לֹא אִירָא, מַה יַּעֲשֶׂה
לִי אָדָם. יהוה לִי בְּעֹזְרָי, וַאֲנִי אֶרְאֶה בְשׂנְאָי. טוֹב לַחֲסוֹת בַּיהוה
מִבְּטֹחַ בָּאָדָם. טוֹב לַחֲסוֹת בַּיהוה מִבְּטֹחַ בִּנְדִיבִים. כָּל גּוֹיִם סְבָבוּנִי
בְּשֵׁם יהוה כִּי אֲמִילַם. סַבּוּנִי גַם סְבָבוּנִי בְּשֵׁם יהוה כִּי אֲמִילַם. סַבּוּנִי
כִדְבֹרִים דֹּעֲכוּ כְּאֵשׁ קוֹצִים, בְּשֵׁם יהוה כִּי אֲמִילַם. דָּחֹה דְחִיתַנִי לִנְפֹּל,
וַיהוה עֲזָרָנִי. עָזִּי וְזִמְרָת יָּה, וַיְהִי לִי לִישׁוּעָה. קוֹל רִנָּה וִישׁוּעָה בְּאָהֳלֵי
צַדִּיקִים, יְמִין יהוה עֹשָׂה חָיִל. יְמִין יהוה רוֹמֵמָה, יְמִין יהוה עֹשָׂה חָיִל.
לֹא אָמוּת כִּי אֶחְיֶה, וַאֲסַפֵּר מַעֲשֵׂי יָּה. יַסֹּר יִסְּרַנִּי יָּה, וְלַמָּוֶת לֹא נְתָנָנִי.

פִּתְחוּ לִי שַׁעֲרֵי צֶדֶק, אָבֹא בָם אוֹדֶה יָּה. זֶה הַשַּׁעַר לַיהוה, צַדִּיקִים
יָבֹאוּ בוֹ. אוֹדְךָ כִּי עֲנִיתָנִי, וַתְּהִי לִי לִישׁוּעָה. אוֹדְךָ כִּי עֲנִיתָנִי וַתְּהִי
לִי לִישׁוּעָה. אֶבֶן מָאֲסוּ הַבּוֹנִים, הָיְתָה לְרֹאשׁ פִּנָּה. אֶבֶן מָאֲסוּ הַבּוֹנִים,
הָיְתָה לְרֹאשׁ פִּנָּה. מֵאֵת יהוה הָיְתָה זֹּאת, הִיא נִפְלָאת בְּעֵינֵינוּ:
מֵאֵת יהוה הָיְתָה זֹּאת, הִיא נִפְלָאת בְּעֵינֵינוּ. זֶה הַיּוֹם עָשָׂה יהוה,
נָגִילָה וְנִשְׂמְחָה בוֹ. זֶה הַיּוֹם עָשָׂה יהוה נָגִילָה וְנִשְׂמְחָה בוֹ.

From the narrows, I called upon the Lord; the Lord answered me by placing me in a great expanse. The Lord is with me; what can man do to me? The Lord is with me among my helpers; I shall see my foes. It is better to seek refuge in the Lord than to trust in man. It is better to seek refuge in the Lord than to trust in princes. All nations have encompassed me; but in the name of the Lord, I routed them. They circled around me, indeed, they circled around me; but in the name of the Lord, I cut them down. They swarmed like bees about me, but they were extinguished like a fire of thorns; but in the name of the Lord, I cut them down. You surely pushed me that I might fall, but the Lord helped me. The Lord is my strength and song; He has become my salvation. The voice of rejoicing and salvation is in the tents of the righteous: "The right hand of the Lord does valiantly. The Lord's right hand is raised in triumph; the Lord's right hand does valiantly!" I shall not die, but live to relate the deeds of the Lord. The Lord has surely punished me, but He has not left me to die.

Open for me the gates of righteousness, that I may enter and praise the Lord. This is the gate of the Lord; the righteous may enter through it. I thank You for You have answered me and have become my salvation. I thank You for You have answered me and have become my salvation. The stone which the builders rejected has become the major cornerstone. The stone which the builders rejected has become the major cornerstone. This is the Lord's doing; it is marvelous in our eyes. This is the Lord's doing; it is marvelous in our eyes. This is the day which the Lord has made; we will be glad and rejoice on it. This is the day which the Lord has made; we will be glad and rejoice on it.

אָנָּא יהוה הוֹשִׁיעָה נָּא:

אָנָּא יהוה הוֹשִׁיעָה נָּא:

אָנָּא יהוה הַצְלִיחָה נָּא:

אָנָּא יהוה הַצְלִיחָה נָּא:

בָּרוּךְ הַבָּא בְּשֵׁם יהוה, בֵּרַכְנוּכֶם מִבֵּית יהוה. בָּרוּךְ הַבָּא בְּשֵׁם יהוה,
בֵּרַכְנוּכֶם מִבֵּית יהוה. אֵל יהוה וַיָּאֶר לָנוּ, אִסְרוּ חַג בַּעֲבֹתִים עַד קַרְנוֹת
הַמִּזְבֵּחַ. אֵל יהוה וַיָּאֶר לָנוּ, אִסְרוּ חַג בַּעֲבֹתִים, עַד קַרְנוֹת הַמִּזְבֵּחַ. אֵלִי
אַתָּה וְאוֹדֶךָּ אֱלֹהַי אֲרוֹמְמֶךָּ. אֵלִי אַתָּה וְאוֹדֶךָּ אֱלֹהַי אֲרוֹמְמֶךָּ: הוֹדוּ לַיהוה
כִּי טוֹב, כִּי לְעוֹלָם חַסְדּוֹ: הוֹדוּ לַיהוה כִּי טוֹב, כִּי לְעוֹלָם חַסְדּוֹ.

יְהַלְלוּךָ יהוה אֱלֹהֵינוּ כָּל מַעֲשֶׂיךָ, וַחֲסִידֶיךָ צַדִּיקִים עוֹשֵׂי רְצוֹנֶךָ, וְכָל
עַמְּךָ בֵּית יִשְׂרָאֵל בְּרִנָּה יוֹדוּ וִיבָרְכוּ וִישַׁבְּחוּ וִיפָאֲרוּ וִירוֹמְמוּ וְיַעֲרִיצוּ
וְיַקְדִּישׁוּ וְיַמְלִיכוּ אֶת שִׁמְךָ מַלְכֵּנוּ, כִּי לְךָ טוֹב לְהוֹדוֹת וּלְשִׁמְךָ נָאֶה לְזַמֵּר,
כִּי מֵעוֹלָם וְעַד עוֹלָם אַתָּה אֵל.

Oh Lord, please save us!

Oh Lord, please save us!

Oh Lord, please let us prosper!

Oh Lord, please let us prosper!

Blessed be he who comes in the name of the Lord; we bless you from the
house of the Lord. Blessed be he who comes in the name of the Lord; we
bless you from the house of the Lord. The Lord is God Who has shown us
light; bind the sacrifice with cords, up to the altar-horns. The Lord is God
Who has shown us light; bind the sacrifice with cords, up to the altar-horns.
You are my God, and I thank You; You are my God, and I will exalt You. You
are my God, and I thank You; You are my God, and I will exalt You. Give
thanks to the Lord, for He is good; for His kindness endures forever. Give
thanks to the Lord, for He is good; for His kindness endures forever.

All Your works praise You, Lord our God; and Your pious followers who
perform Your will, and all Your people the house of Israel, thank, and bless,
and praise, and glorify, and extol, and exalt, revere, sanctify, and coronate
Your name, our King. To You it is fitting to give thanks, and unto Your name
it is proper to sing praises, for You are God eternal.

כִּי לְעוֹלָם חַסְדּוֹ:	הוֹדוּ לַיהוה כִּי טוֹב,
כִּי לְעוֹלָם חַסְדּוֹ:	הוֹדוּ לֵאלֹהֵי הָאֱלֹהִים,
כִּי לְעוֹלָם חַסְדּוֹ:	הוֹדוּ לַאֲדֹנֵי הָאֲדֹנִים,
כִּי לְעוֹלָם חַסְדּוֹ:	לְעֹשֵׂה נִפְלָאוֹת גְּדֹלוֹת לְבַדּוֹ,
כִּי לְעוֹלָם חַסְדּוֹ:	לְעֹשֵׂה הַשָּׁמַיִם בִּתְבוּנָה,
כִּי לְעוֹלָם חַסְדּוֹ:	לְרוֹקַע הָאָרֶץ עַל הַמָּיִם,
כִּי לְעוֹלָם חַסְדּוֹ:	לְעֹשֵׂה אוֹרִים גְּדֹלִים,
כִּי לְעוֹלָם חַסְדּוֹ:	אֶת הַשֶּׁמֶשׁ לְמֶמְשֶׁלֶת בַּיּוֹם,
כִּי לְעוֹלָם חַסְדּוֹ:	אֶת הַיָּרֵחַ וְכוֹכָבִים לְמֶמְשְׁלוֹת בַּלָּיְלָה,
כִּי לְעוֹלָם חַסְדּוֹ:	לְמַכֵּה מִצְרַיִם בִּבְכוֹרֵיהֶם,
כִּי לְעוֹלָם חַסְדּוֹ:	וַיּוֹצֵא יִשְׂרָאֵל מִתּוֹכָם,
כִּי לְעוֹלָם חַסְדּוֹ:	בְּיָד חֲזָקָה וּבִזְרוֹעַ נְטוּיָה,
כִּי לְעוֹלָם חַסְדּוֹ:	לְגֹזֵר יַם סוּף לִגְזָרִים,

Give thanks to the Lord, for He is good, For His kindness endures forever.

Give thanks to the God above gods, For His kindness endures forever.

Give thanks to the Lord of lords, For His kindness endures forever.

To Him Who alone does great wonders, For His kindness endures forever.

To Him Who made the heavens with understanding, For His kindness endures forever.

To Him Who stretched the earth over the waters, For His kindness endures forever.

To Him Who made the great lights, For His kindness endures forever.

The sun to reign by day, For His kindness endures forever.

The moon and the stars to reign by night, For His kindness endures forever.

To Him Who smote Egypt in their firstborn, For His kindness endures forever.

And took Israel out from among them, For His kindness endures forever.

With a strong hand and an outstretched arm, For His kindness endures forever.

To Him who parted the Reed Sea, For His kindness endures forever.

כִּי לְעוֹלָם חַסְדּוֹ:	וְהֶעֱבִיר יִשְׂרָאֵל בְּתוֹכוֹ,
כִּי לְעוֹלָם חַסְדּוֹ:	וְנִעֵר פַּרְעֹה וְחֵילוֹ בְיַם סוּף,
כִּי לְעוֹלָם חַסְדּוֹ:	לְמוֹלִיךְ עַמּוֹ בַּמִּדְבָּר,
כִּי לְעוֹלָם חַסְדּוֹ:	לְמַכֵּה מְלָכִים גְּדֹלִים,
כִּי לְעוֹלָם חַסְדּוֹ:	וַיַּהֲרֹג מְלָכִים אַדִּירִים,
כִּי לְעוֹלָם חַסְדּוֹ:	לְסִיחוֹן מֶלֶךְ הָאֱמֹרִי,
כִּי לְעוֹלָם חַסְדּוֹ:	וּלְעוֹג מֶלֶךְ הַבָּשָׁן,
כִּי לְעוֹלָם חַסְדּוֹ:	וְנָתַן אַרְצָם לְנַחֲלָה,
כִּי לְעוֹלָם חַסְדּוֹ:	נַחֲלָה לְיִשְׂרָאֵל עַבְדּוֹ,
כִּי לְעוֹלָם חַסְדּוֹ:	שֶׁבְּשִׁפְלֵנוּ זָכַר לָנוּ,
כִּי לְעוֹלָם חַסְדּוֹ:	וַיִּפְרְקֵנוּ מִצָּרֵינוּ,
כִּי לְעוֹלָם חַסְדּוֹ:	נוֹתֵן לֶחֶם לְכָל בָּשָׂר,
כִּי לְעוֹלָם חַסְדּוֹ:	הוֹדוּ לְאֵל הַשָּׁמָיִם,

And caused Israel to pass through it, For His kindness endures forever.

And threw Pharaoh and his host in the Reed Sea, For His kindness endures forever.

To Him Who led His people through the wilderness, For His kindness endures forever.

To Him Who smote great kings, For His kindness endures forever.

And slew mighty kings, For His kindness endures forever.

Sihon, king of the Amorites, For His kindness endures forever.

And Og, king of Bashan, For His kindness endures forever.

And gave their land as an inheritance, For His kindness endures forever.

An inheritance to Israel His servant, For His kindness endures forever.

Who remembered us in our low state, For His kindness endures forever.

And released us from our foes, For His kindness endures forever.

Who gives food to all creatures, For His kindness endures forever.

Give thanks to God of all heaven, For His kindness endures forever.

נִשְׁמַת כָּל חַי, תְּבָרֵךְ אֶת שִׁמְךָ יהוה אֱלֹהֵינוּ. וְרוּחַ כָּל בָּשָׂר, תְּפָאֵר וּתְרוֹמֵם זִכְרְךָ מַלְכֵּנוּ תָּמִיד, מִן הָעוֹלָם וְעַד הָעוֹלָם אַתָּה אֵל. וּמִבַּלְעָדֶיךָ אֵין לָנוּ מֶלֶךְ גּוֹאֵל וּמוֹשִׁיעַ, פּוֹדֶה וּמַצִּיל וּמְפַרְנֵס וּמְרַחֵם, בְּכָל עֵת צָרָה וְצוּקָה. אֵין לָנוּ מֶלֶךְ אֶלָּא אָתָּה: אֱלֹהֵי הָרִאשׁוֹנִים וְהָאַחֲרוֹנִים, אֱלוֹהַּ כָּל בְּרִיּוֹת, אֲדוֹן כָּל תּוֹלָדוֹת, הַמְהֻלָּל בְּרֹב הַתִּשְׁבָּחוֹת, הַמְנַהֵג עוֹלָמוֹ בְּחֶסֶד, וּבְרִיּוֹתָיו בְּרַחֲמִים. וַיהוה לֹא יָנוּם וְלֹא יִישָׁן, הַמְעוֹרֵר יְשֵׁנִים וְהַמֵּקִיץ נִרְדָּמִים, וְהַמֵּשִׂיחַ אִלְּמִים, וְהַמַּתִּיר אֲסוּרִים, וְהַסּוֹמֵךְ נוֹפְלִים, וְהַזּוֹקֵף כְּפוּפִים, לְךָ לְבַדְּךָ אֲנַחְנוּ מוֹדִים.

אִלּוּ פִינוּ מָלֵא שִׁירָה כַּיָּם, וּלְשׁוֹנֵנוּ רִנָּה כַּהֲמוֹן גַּלָּיו, וְשִׂפְתוֹתֵינוּ שֶׁבַח כְּמֶרְחֲבֵי רָקִיעַ, וְעֵינֵינוּ מְאִירוֹת כַּשֶּׁמֶשׁ וְכַיָּרֵחַ, וְיָדֵינוּ פְרוּשׂוֹת כְּנִשְׁרֵי שָׁמָיִם, וְרַגְלֵינוּ קַלּוֹת כָּאַיָּלוֹת, אֵין אֲנַחְנוּ מַסְפִּיקִים, לְהוֹדוֹת לְךָ יהוה אֱלֹהֵינוּ וֵאלֹהֵי אֲבוֹתֵינוּ, וּלְבָרֵךְ אֶת שְׁמֶךָ עַל אַחַת מֵאֶלֶף אֶלֶף אַלְפֵי אֲלָפִים וְרִבֵּי רְבָבוֹת פְּעָמִים, הַטּוֹבוֹת שֶׁעָשִׂיתָ עִם אֲבוֹתֵינוּ וְעִמָּנוּ. מִמִּצְרַיִם גְּאַלְתָּנוּ יהוה אֱלֹהֵינוּ, וּמִבֵּית עֲבָדִים פְּדִיתָנוּ, בְּרָעָב זַנְתָּנוּ, וּבְשָׂבָע כִּלְכַּלְתָּנוּ, מֵחֶרֶב הִצַּלְתָּנוּ, וּמִדֶּבֶר מִלַּטְתָּנוּ, וּמֵחֳלָיִם רָעִים

The soul of every living being shall bless Your name, Lord, our God. The spirit of all flesh shall ever glorify and exalt Your remembrance, our King. Throughout eternity You are God. Aside from You, we have no king who redeems and saves, ransoms and rescues, sustains and shows mercy in all times of trouble and distress. We have no king but You, God of the first and of the last, God of all creatures, Master of all generations, One coronated with a multitude of praises, He Who guides His world with kindness and His creatures with mercy. The Lord neither slumbers nor sleeps; He rouses those who sleep and wakens those who slumber; He enables the speechless to speak and loosens the bonds of the captives; He supports those who are fallen and raises those who are bowed down. To You alone we give thanks.

Were our mouth filled with song as the ocean, and our tongue with joy as the endless waves; were our lips full of praise as the wide heavens, and our eyes shining like the sun or the moon; were our hands spread out in prayer as the eagles of the sky and our feet running as swiftly as the deer--we should still be unable to thank You and bless Your name, Lord our God and God of our fathers, for one of the thousands and even myriads of favors which You have bestowed on our fathers and on us. You have liberated us from Egypt, Lord our God, and redeemed us from the house of slavery. You have fed us in famine and sustained us with plenty. You have saved us from the sword, helped us to escape the plague, and spared us from

וְנֶאֱמָנִים דְּלִיתָנוּ: עַד הֵנָּה עֲזָרוּנוּ רַחֲמֶיךָ, וְלֹא עֲזָבוּנוּ חֲסָדֶיךָ וְאַל תִּטְּשֵׁנוּ יהוה אֱלֹהֵינוּ לָנֶצַח. עַל כֵּן אֵבָרִים שֶׁפִּלַּגְתָּ בָּנוּ, וְרוּחַ וּנְשָׁמָה שֶׁנָּפַחְתָּ בְּאַפֵּינוּ, וְלָשׁוֹן אֲשֶׁר שַׂמְתָּ בְּפִינוּ, הֵן הֵם יוֹדוּ וִיבָרְכוּ וִישַׁבְּחוּ וִיפָאֲרוּ וִירוֹמְמוּ וְיַעֲרִיצוּ וְיַקְדִּישׁוּ וְיַמְלִיכוּ אֶת שִׁמְךָ מַלְכֵּנוּ, כִּי כָל פֶּה לְךָ יוֹדֶה, וְכָל לָשׁוֹן לְךָ תִּשָּׁבַע, וְכָל בֶּרֶךְ לְךָ תִכְרַע, וְכָל קוֹמָה לְפָנֶיךָ תִשְׁתַּחֲוֶה, וְכָל לְבָבוֹת יִירָאוּךָ, וְכָל קֶרֶב וּכְלָיוֹת יְזַמְּרוּ לִשְׁמֶךָ. כַּדָּבָר שֶׁכָּתוּב, כָּל עַצְמוֹתַי תֹּאמַרְנָה יהוה מִי כָמוֹךָ. מַצִּיל עָנִי מֵחָזָק מִמֶּנּוּ, וְעָנִי וְאֶבְיוֹן מִגֹּזְלוֹ: מִי יִדְמֶה לָּךְ, וּמִי יִשְׁוֶה לָּךְ וּמִי יַעֲרָךְ לָךְ: הָאֵל הַגָּדוֹל הַגִּבּוֹר וְהַנּוֹרָא, אֵל עֶלְיוֹן קֹנֵה שָׁמַיִם וָאָרֶץ: נְהַלֶּלְךָ וּנְשַׁבֵּחֲךָ וּנְפָאֶרְךָ וּנְבָרֵךְ אֶת־שֵׁם קָדְשֶׁךָ. כָּאָמוּר, לְדָוִד, בָּרְכִי נַפְשִׁי אֶת יהוה, וְכָל קְרָבַי אֶת שֵׁם קָדְשׁוֹ:

הָאֵל בְּתַעֲצֻמוֹת עֻזֶּךָ, הַגָּדוֹל בִּכְבוֹד שְׁמֶךָ. הַגִּבּוֹר לָנֶצַח וְהַנּוֹרָא בְּנוֹרְאוֹתֶיךָ. הַמֶּלֶךְ הַיּוֹשֵׁב עַל כִּסֵּא רָם וְנִשָּׂא:

---

severe and enduring diseases. Until now, Your mercy has helped us, and Your kindness has not forsaken us; may You, Lord our God, never abandon us. Therefore, the limbs which You have given us, the spirit and soul which You have breathed into our nostrils, and the tongue which You have placed in our mouth, shall all thank and bless, praise and glorify, exalt and revere, sanctify and coronate Your name, our King. For to You, every mouth shall offer thanks; every tongue shall vow allegiance; every knee shall bend, and all who stand erect shall bow. All hearts shall revere You, and men's inner beings and organs shall sing to Your name, as it is written: "all my bones shall say: Oh Lord, who is like You? You save the poor man from one that is stronger, the poor and needy from one who would rob him." Who may be likened to You? Who is equal to You? Who can be compared to You? Oh great, mighty and revered God, supreme God is the master of heaven and earth. Let us praise, acclaim and glorify You and bless Your holy name, as it is said: "A Psalm of David: Bless the Lord, Oh my soul, and let my whole inner being bless His holy name."

Oh God in Your mighty acts of power, great in the honor of Your name, powerful forever and revered for Your awe-inspiring acts, Oh King seated upon a high and lofty throne!

שׁוֹכֵן עַד, מָרוֹם וְקָדוֹשׁ שְׁמוֹ: וְכָתוּב, רַנְּנוּ צַדִּיקִים בַּיהוה, לַיְשָׁרִים נָאוָה תְהִלָּה. בְּפִי יְשָׁרִים תִּתְהַלָּל. וּבְדִבְרֵי צַדִּיקִים תִּתְבָּרַךְ. וּבִלְשׁוֹן חֲסִידִים תִּתְרוֹמָם. וּבְקֶרֶב קְדוֹשִׁים תִּתְקַדָּשׁ:

וּבְמַקְהֲלוֹת רִבְבוֹת עַמְּךָ בֵּית יִשְׂרָאֵל, בְּרִנָּה יִתְפָּאַר שִׁמְךָ מַלְכֵּנוּ, בְּכָל דּוֹר וָדוֹר, שֶׁכֵּן חוֹבַת כָּל הַיְצוּרִים, לְפָנֶיךָ יהוה אֱלֹהֵינוּ, וֵאלֹהֵי אֲבוֹתֵינוּ, לְהוֹדוֹת לְהַלֵּל לְשַׁבֵּחַ לְפָאֵר לְרוֹמֵם לְהַדֵּר לְבָרֵךְ לְעַלֵּה וּלְקַלֵּס, עַל כָּל דִּבְרֵי שִׁירוֹת וְתִשְׁבְּחוֹת דָּוִד בֶּן יִשַׁי עַבְדְּךָ מְשִׁיחֶךָ:

יִשְׁתַּבַּח שִׁמְךָ לָעַד מַלְכֵּנוּ, הָאֵל הַמֶּלֶךְ הַגָּדוֹל וְהַקָּדוֹשׁ בַּשָּׁמַיִם וּבָאָרֶץ. כִּי לְךָ נָאֶה, יהוה אֱלֹהֵינוּ וֵאלֹהֵי אֲבוֹתֵינוּ: שִׁיר וּשְׁבָחָה, הַלֵּל וְזִמְרָה, עֹז וּמֶמְשָׁלָה, נֶצַח, גְּדֻלָּה וּגְבוּרָה, תְּהִלָּה וְתִפְאֶרֶת, קְדֻשָּׁה וּמַלְכוּת, בְּרָכוֹת וְהוֹדָאוֹת מֵעַתָּה וְעַד עוֹלָם. בָּרוּךְ אַתָּה יהוה, אֵל מֶלֶךְ גָּדוֹל בַּתִּשְׁבָּחוֹת, אֵל הַהוֹדָאוֹת, אֲדוֹן הַנִּפְלָאוֹת, הַבּוֹחֵר בְּשִׁירֵי זִמְרָה, מֶלֶךְ, אֵל, חֵי הָעוֹלָמִים.

He Who abides forever, exalted and holy is His name. And it is written: "Rejoice in the Lord, you righteous; it is pleasant for the upright to give praise." By the mouth of the upright You shall be praised. And be blessed. And by the words of the righteous You shall be blessed. And by the tongue of the pious You shall be exalted. And in the midst of the holy You shall be sanctified.

And in the assemblies of the multitudes of Your people, the house of Israel, with joyous song shall Your name, our King, be glorified in every generation. For it is the duty of all creatures before You Lord, our God, and God of our fathers, to thank, praise, laud, extol, exalt, adore, bless elevate, and adore You; even beyond the songs and praises of David the son of Jesse, Your anointed servant.

Praised be Your name forever, our King, God, King, great and holy in heaven and on earth; for to You, Lord our God, it is fitting to render song and praise, hallel and psalms, power and dominion, victory, glory and might, praise and beauty, holiness and sovereignty, blessings and thanks from now and forever. God, You are the source of blessing, God, King, great in praises, God of thanks, Master of wonders, Who makes choice of song and psalm, King, God, the Life of all worlds.

The blessing over the wine is recited, and the fourth cup is drunk while reclining to the left side. Preferably, one should drink the entire cup. At the least, most of the cup should be drunk.

בָּרוּךְ אַתָּה יְהוָה, אֱלֹהֵינוּ מֶלֶךְ הָעוֹלָם, בּוֹרֵא פְּרִי הַגָּפֶן:

בָּרוּךְ אַתָּה יְהוָה אֱלֹהֵינוּ מֶלֶךְ הָעוֹלָם עַל הַגֶּפֶן וְעַל פְּרִי הַגֶּפֶן. וְעַל תְּנוּבַת הַשָּׂדֶה, וְעַל אֶרֶץ חֶמְדָּה טוֹבָה וּרְחָבָה, שֶׁרָצִיתָ וְהִנְחַלְתָּ לַאֲבוֹתֵינוּ, לֶאֱכוֹל מִפִּרְיָהּ וְלִשְׂבּוֹעַ מִטּוּבָהּ. רַחֶם (נָא) יְהוָה אֱלֹהֵינוּ עַל יִשְׂרָאֵל עַמֶּךְ, וְעַל יְרוּשָׁלַיִם עִירֶךָ, וְעַל צִיּוֹן מִשְׁכַּן כְּבוֹדֶךָ, וְעַל מִזְבְּחֶךָ וְעַל הֵיכָלֶךָ. וּבְנֵה יְרוּשָׁלַיִם עִיר הַקֹּדֶשׁ בִּמְהֵרָה בְיָמֵינוּ, וְהַעֲלֵנוּ לְתוֹכָהּ, וְשַׂמְּחֵנוּ בְּבִנְיָנָהּ וְנֹאכַל מִפִּרְיָהּ וְנִשְׂבַּע מִטּוּבָהּ, וּנְבָרֶכְךָ עָלֶיהָ בִּקְדֻשָּׁה וּבְטָהֳרָה

On Friday night add: (וּרְצֵה וְהַחֲלִיצֵנוּ בְּיוֹם הַשַּׁבָּת הַזֶּה.)

וְשַׂמְּחֵנוּ בְּיוֹם חַג הַמַּצּוֹת הַזֶּה. כִּי אַתָּה יְהוָה טוֹב וּמֵטִיב לַכֹּל, וְנוֹדֶה לְּךָ עַל הָאָרֶץ וְעַל פְּרִי הַגֶּפֶן. בָּרוּךְ אַתָּה יְהוָה, עַל הָאָרֶץ וְעַל פְּרִי הַגֶּפֶן:

The blessing over the wine is recited, and the fourth cup is drunk while reclining to the left side. Preferably, one should drink the entire cup. At the least, most of the cup should be drunk.

God, You are the source of blessing, Our God, King of the universe, Who creates the fruit of the vine.

God, You are the source of blessing, Our God, King of the universe, for the vine and its fruit, and for the produce of the field, for the beautiful and spacious land which in Your favor You gave to our fathers as a heritage to eat of its fruit and to enjoy its goodness. Have mercy, Lord our God, on Israel Your people, on Jerusalem Your city, on Zion the abode of Your glory, on Your altar and on Your Temple. And rebuild Jerusalem, the holy city, speedily in our days. And bring us into its midst and cheer us with its restoration; that we may eat of its fruit and enjoy of its goodness; and may we bless You for it in holiness and purity.

On Friday night add:

(And favor us and strengthen us on this Shabbat day.)

And grant us happiness on this Feast of Matzot; For You, O Lord, are good and beneficent to all, and we thank You for the land and the fruit of the vine. God, You are the source of blessing, for the land and for the fruit of the vine.

L'SHANA HABAAH B'YERUSHALAYIM NEXT YEAR IN JERUSALEM

Twice a year, every year, at the conclusion of the Pesach Seder and on Yom Kippur at the Neilah service, the Jew proclaims the immortal words: "Next year in Jerusalem." Our tradition speaks of the "Jerusalem above" and the "Jerusalem below ..." , the heavenly Jerusalem and the earthly Jerusalem. It is in Jerusalem where heaven and earth – the physical and the spiritual – combine together as one. And it is this very same Jerusalem that is the source of so much conflict and misunderstanding. Jerusalem, Israel's capital, is the only capital in the world that is not internationally recognized as its country's capital. Everyone lays claim to Jerusalem; Jews, Christians and Muslims claim it is holy to them. There is no way to measure holiness, but the fact is, over the centuries Rome, not Jerusalem, became the center of Christianity. Mecca and Medina, not Jerusalem, became the center of Islam. Only the Jew continued to hope and pray and proclaim, "Next year in Jerusalem."

Perhaps the most upsetting claim about Jerusalem is the charge by some who say that there is no basis for the Jewish claim to Jerusalem. The Palestinian Mufti in Jerusalem is quoted as saying, "There is not even the smallest indication of the existence of a Jewish temple on this place in the past. In the whole city there is not even a single stone indicating Jewish history. It is the art of the Jews to deceive the world. There is not a single stone in the Wailing Wall relating to Jewish history. They cannot legitimately claim it, either religiously nor historically." In a televised interview, Yassir Arafat was quoted as saying, "Let me tell you something. The issue of Jerusalem is not just a Palestinian issue, it is a Palestinian/Arab/Islamic and Christian issue." Asked by the interviewer if one could also say it is a Jewish issue, Arafat replied, "No. Until now all the excavations that have been carried out have failed to prove the location of the temple."

But what about:

- The fact that for 2000 years Jews in every generation pledged, "If I forget thee O Jerusalem, let my right hand wither . . ."

- The fact that Jerusalem is mentioned 750 times in our Bible and not once in the Koran . . .

- The fact that when it was ruled by Byzantines and Arabs and Romans and Syrians and Crusaders and Greeks and Kurds and Mongols and Tartars and Turks – none of them made it their capital. Only to the Jews was this land sacred . . .

- The fact that before 1967 when it was under Arab rule, not one leader of a single Arab country, not one Foreign Minister, ever came to Jerusalem to pray, and when Muslims do pray they turn their backs on Jerusalem . . .

- The fact that during that period of time the Arabs refused a Jew the right to step into the Old City, overturned tombstones on the Mount of Olives, using them for latrines, and destroyed the 24 synagogues in the Old City, dynamiting them one by one . . . and no one said a thing . . .

- And the fact that at the end of every Yom Kippur and at the end of every Pesach Seder, only we as Jews proclaim, "Next year in Jerusalem . . ."

All this means nothing! It means nothing to the Arabs who go on insisting that Jerusalem was never home for the Jewish people. How do you explain it? How do you explain Arab insistence that the temple was not in Jerusalem and the Jews have no claims to Jerusalem, when that goes against everything that history tells us. Elie Wiesel beautifully speaks of Jerusalem this way: "Forever inherent in my Jewishness, it is at the center of my commitments and my dreams.".... "It is the national landmark of our tradition, it represents our collective soul. It is Jerusalem that binds one Jew to another." Jerusalem was never ours? How do you explain the Arab claim?

It all boils down to the words of Iranian President Mahmoud Ahmadinejad, who has called for the destruction of Israel and for the

Jews living there to return to the Europe they came from. According to Mr. Ahmadinejad and many others, it is only after the Holocaust that Europe, feeling guilty, took the homeless, displaced Jews and put them in a country to which they had no historic claim. So let them go back to where they came from. These words lose all meaning when it is recognized that 3000 years ago King David established Jerusalem as the capital of Israel, and that there has been a Jewish presence there ever since, including both temples.

How sad it is that not only many Arabs, but some Jews, don't take the Jewish claim to Jerusalem seriously. More American Jews have visited Acapulco than Jerusalem. And perhaps even worse: a substantial number of Israelis haven't been to Jerusalem! Jerusalem was given to the Jewish people by God, not by international guarantees. Our claims to Israel and Jerusalem are based on the Bible, not the Balfour Declaration. We must remind ourselves that we as Jews are living in historic times and we must not take that for granted.

Rabbi Yehudah Amital has pointed out that in the Book of Zechariah, we find the immortal words of the prophet, "Thus says the Lord of Hosts, 'Old men and old women shall yet again dwell in the streets of Jerusalem and every man with his staff in his hand because of his old age, and the streets of the city shall be full of boys and girls playing in the streets'. Thus, says the Lord of Hosts, 'If it will be wondrous in the eyes of the remnant of this nation in those days, it will also be wondrous in my eyes,' says the Lord of Hosts." What is the prophet telling us? That after the first temple was destroyed, Jerusalem was desolate for 70 years, and now normal life had returned to its streets. That, says the prophet, is considered wondrous in God's eyes. If it was considered wondrous in God's eyes for the people to return to Jerusalem after 70 years, what should we say today after 2000 years? Think about it! Three books of the prophets – Chagai, Zechariah and Malachi – and two from the later writings – Ezra and Nechemia – deal with a total of 40,000 Jews living in Israel. Those were all that remained – 40,000. And today, thanks to the grace of God, we have merited to see 6 million Jews in Israel. Is that not wondrous? Is it possible not to see the great hand of God in our day, with old men and women walking the streets of Jerusalem after 2000 years?

All this means nothing to the Arabs who insist that it was never ours. Perhaps even worse, it seems to mean nothing to many Christians who, upon hearing the Arab claims that there was never a temple in Jerusalem, do not raise their voice and ask, "Then where did Jesus walk?" And perhaps worst of all, it seems to mean little to the majority of Jews in the world today who have never visited Jerusalem. We are the first generation in 2000 years of our people who are able to come and visit and pray in Jerusalem. Every Muslim and Christian must come to accept this and every Jew must come to appreciate it.

- When you say "Next year in Jerusalem," do you really mean it?
- Do you really care about Israel's destiny?
- Do your children?
- As much as you?

נִרְצָה

חֲסַל סִדּוּר פֶּסַח כְּהִלְכָתוֹ,
כְּכָל מִשְׁפָּטוֹ וְחֻקָּתוֹ.
כַּאֲשֶׁר זָכִינוּ לְסַדֵּר אוֹתוֹ,
כֵּן נִזְכֶּה לַעֲשׂוֹתוֹ.
זָךְ שׁוֹכֵן מְעוֹנָה,
קוֹמֵם קְהַל עֲדַת מִי מָנָה.
בְּקָרוֹב נַהֵל נִטְעֵי כַנָּה,
פְּדוּיִם לְצִיּוֹן בְּרִנָּה.

לְשָׁנָה הַבָּאָה בִּירוּשָׁלָיִם!

On the second night of Passover, those who have not counted the omer or who customarily count it during the Seder say the following:

בָּרוּךְ אַתָּה יהוה אֱלֹהֵינוּ מֶלֶךְ הָעוֹלָם, אֲשֶׁר קִדְּשָׁנוּ בְּמִצְוֹתָיו וְצִוָּנוּ עַל סְפִירַת הָעוֹמֶר.

הַיּוֹם יוֹם אֶחָד בָּעוֹמֶר.

Nirtzah

The Seder now concludes according to its Halacha, Complete in all its laws and ordinances. Just as we were privileged to arrange it, So may we be granted to perform it. O Pure One who dwells in the heights above, Establish us as a countless people (once again), Speedily guide the offshoots of the plants Israel redeemed, To Zion with joyous song.

NEXT YEAR IN JERUSALEM!

On the second night of Passover, those who have not counted the omer or who customarily count it during the Seder say the following:

God, You are the source of all blessing, our God, King of the universe Who has sanctified us with His commandments and has commanded us regarding the counting of the omer.

Today is the first day in the omer.

U'VCHEIN VAYHI BACHATZI HA-LAILAH
AND SO IT WAS IN THE MIDDLE OF THE NIGHT

This poem describes the many events that took place on the eve of the 15th day of Nisan. While we commemorate that day as being the time of the exodus from Egypt, a lot more occurred on this day, including the death of Haman, the conquest of Jericho, God's visit to Abraham, the defeat of Sennacherib. The 15th day of Nisan is considered *"mazeldik"* – a lucky one – in the Jewish calendar. So much so that the prayer we recite before going to bed is abbreviated on the Seder night, for this night is considered a *"leil shemurim"* – a night of special Divine Protection.

While the 15th of Nisan is considered a "lucky day" in the Jewish calendar, the 9th day of Av is considered a day of misfortune, commemorating as it does the day on which both temples in Jerusalem were destroyed, as well as other tragic moments in Jewish history. These include the day on which it was decreed that the generation of the Jews in the wilderness would not enter the Promised Land, the day on which the great city of Betar was conquered, and the day on which Jews were exiled from Spain. According to Jewish tradition, on the 9th of Av – indeed on the days leading up to the 9th of Av – one is supposed to avoid going to court or having a medical procedure because this is an "unlucky" time for the Jews.

The idea that some days are lucky and some are not would seem to indicate that some things are in the "stars"; indeed the word "mazel," which we translate as "luck," also means "constellation." According to the Zohar, the Book of Kabbalah, "All the stars and constellations in the heavens were appointed to be rulers over the world. There is not a single blade of grass in the entire world over which a star or planet does not preside."

When it was revealed that when Nancy Reagan was First Lady, many major decisions she and her husband made were first cleared in advance with a woman in San Francisco who drew up horoscopes to make certain that the planets were in a favorable alignment for the enterprise, people thought she was crazy. And yet, if you look in the Bible, there are 23,144 verses. Of these verses, 866 refer to the heavens, sun, moon, stars, constellations, host of heaven and planets. Fully 74% of these verses refer to these heavenly bodies as being directly involved in making manifest the will of God, either as omens, witnesses or as active agents.

The rabbis in the Talmud made a horoscope for every day of the week and assigned a sign of the zodiac to each one of the Hebrew months, as can be seen in ancient mosaics found in synagogues in Israel. For example, the sign for the Hebrew month of Sivan is Gemini, the Twins, the month when the "twin tablets" were given on Mt. Sinai and, according to tradition, when the twins Jacob and Esau were born.

?
• Do you believe in astrology?
• Do you think some days are "luckier" than others?
• Do you read your horoscope in the paper, or do you agree with Maimonides who considered astrology "a disease, not a science?"
• Do you think some things are just a matter of fate?

וּבְכֵן "וַיְהִי בַּחֲצִי הַלַּיְלָה."

אָז רוֹב נִסִּים הִפְלֵאתָ בַּלַּיְלָה,
בְּרֹאשׁ אַשְׁמוּרוֹת זֶה הַלַּיְלָה,
גֵּר צֶדֶק נִצַּחְתּוֹ כְּנֶחֱלַק לוֹ לַיְלָה,
וַיְהִי בַּחֲצִי הַלַּיְלָה.

דַּנְתָּ מֶלֶךְ גְּרָר בַּחֲלוֹם הַלַּיְלָה,
הִפְחַדְתָּ אֲרַמִּי בְּאֶמֶשׁ לַיְלָה,
וַיָּשַׂר יִשְׂרָאֵל לְמַלְאָךְ וַיּוּכַל לוֹ לַיְלָה,
וַיְהִי בַּחֲצִי הַלַּיְלָה.

זֶרַע בְּכוֹרֵי פַתְרוֹס מָחַצְתָּ בַּחֲצִי הַלַּיְלָה,
חֵילָם לֹא מָצְאוּ בְּקוּמָם בַּלַּיְלָה,
טִיסַת נְגִיד חֲרֹשֶׁת סִלִּיתָ בְּכוֹכְבֵי לַיְלָה,
וַיְהִי בַּחֲצִי הַלַּיְלָה.

יָעַץ מְחָרֵף לְנוֹפֵף אִוּוּי, הוֹבַשְׁתָּ פְגָרָיו בַּלַּיְלָה,
כָּרַע בֵּל וּמַצָּבוֹ בְּאִישׁוֹן לַיְלָה,

AND THUS "IT CAME TO PASS AT MIDNIGHT."

You performed most wonders at night,
In the early watches of this night; The righteous convert,
Avraham, did You cause to triumph at night;
It came to pass at midnight.

You judged Grar's king, (Avimelech), in a dream by night;
You frightened Laban in the dark of night;
Israel overcame an angel and won by night;
It came to pass at midnight.

You crushed Egypt's (Pharaoh's) firstborn at midnight;
Their strength, they found not when they rose at night;
Sisera, prince of Harashet, did You rout through stars of the night;
It came to pass at midnight.

You disgraced Sanncherib, the blasphemer, by night;
Babylon's idol fell in the dark of night;

לְאִישׁ חֲמוּדוֹת נִגְלָה רָז חֲזוֹת לַיְלָה,
וַיְהִי בַּחֲצִי הַלַּיְלָה.

מִשְׁתַּכֵּר בִּכְלֵי קֹדֶשׁ נֶהֱרַג בּוֹ בַּלַּיְלָה,
נוֹשַׁע מִבּוֹר אֲרָיוֹת פּוֹתֵר בִּעֲתוּתֵי לַיְלָה.
שִׂנְאָה נָטַר אֲגָגִי וְכָתַב סְפָרִים לַיְלָה,
וַיְהִי בַּחֲצִי הַלַּיְלָה.

עוֹרַרְתָּ נִצְחֲךָ עָלָיו בְּנֶדֶד שְׁנַת לַיְלָה,
פּוּרָה תִדְרוֹךְ לְשׁוֹמֵר מַה מִּלַּיְלָה,
צָרַח כַּשּׁוֹמֵר וְשָׂח אָתָא בֹקֶר וְגַם לַיְלָה,
וַיְהִי בַּחֲצִי הַלַּיְלָה.

קָרֵב יוֹם אֲשֶׁר הוּא לֹא יוֹם וְלֹא לַיְלָה,
רָם הוֹדַע כִּי לְךָ הַיּוֹם אַף לְךָ הַלַּיְלָה,
שׁוֹמְרִים הַפְקֵד לְעִירְךָ כָּל הַיּוֹם וְכָל הַלַּיְלָה,
תָּאִיר כְּאוֹר יוֹם חֶשְׁכַּת לַיְלָה,
וַיְהִי בַּחֲצִי הַלַּיְלָה:

Daniel was shown the secret of the king's dream of the night;
It came to pass at midnight.

Belshazzar, who became drunk from drinking from the Temple's vessel, was killed that same night;
Daniel who was saved from the lion's den interpreted the visions of night;
Hateful Haman the Agagite wrote letters in the night;
It came to pass at midnight.

You triumphed against Haman in the king's sleepless night;
Trample the wine press and aid those who ask; "What of the night?"
The watchman responds: "Morning comes after night;"
It came to pass at midnight.

Hasten the eternal day which is not really day or night;
Exalted One, proclaim that You are day and night;
Set guards about Your city all day and night;
Brighten as day the darkness of the night;
It came to pass at midnight.

On the second night, recite:

וּבְכֵן "וַאֲמַרְתֶּם זֶבַח פֶּסַח."

אֹמֶץ גְּבוּרוֹתֶיךָ הִפְלֵאתָ בַּפֶּסַח,
בְּרֹאשׁ כָּל מוֹעֲדוֹת נִשֵּׂאתָ פֶּסַח,
גִּלִּיתָ לָאֶזְרָחִי חֲצוֹת לֵיל פֶּסַח,
וַאֲמַרְתֶּם זֶבַח פֶּסַח.

דְּלָתָיו דָּפַקְתָּ כְּחֹם הַיּוֹם בַּפֶּסַח,
הִסְעִיד נוֹצְצִים עֻגוֹת מַצּוֹת בַּפֶּסַח,
וְאֶל הַבָּקָר רָץ זֵכֶר לְשׁוֹר עֵרֶךְ פֶּסַח,
וַאֲמַרְתֶּם זֶבַח פֶּסַח.

זֹעֲמוּ סְדוֹמִים וְלֹהֲטוּ בָּאֵשׁ בַּפֶּסַח,
חֻלַּץ לוֹט מֵהֶם, וּמַצּוֹת אָפָה בְּקֵץ פֶּסַח,
טִאטֵאתָ אַדְמַת מֹף וְנֹף בְּעָבְרְךָ בַּפֶּסַח,
וַאֲמַרְתֶּם זֶבַח פֶּסַח.

יָהּ, רֹאשׁ כָּל אוֹן מָחַצְתָּ בְּלֵיל שִׁמּוּר פֶּסַח,
כַּבִּיר, עַל בֵּן בְּכוֹר פָּסַחְתָּ בְּדַם פֶּסַח,

On the second night, recite:

And Thus: "And you shall say: It is the Pesach sacrifice."

Your wondrous powers did You display on Pesach;
Chief of all feasts did You make Pesach;
You did reveal Yourself to Abraham on the midnight of Pesach;
And you shall say: It is the Pesach sacrifice.

To his door did You knock at noon on Pesach;
With matzot, he served angels on Pesach;
To the herd, he ran for the ox recalling Joseph on Pesach;
And you shall say: It is the Pesach sacrifice.

The men of S'dom were burned in wrath on Pesach;
Lot was saved, he baked matzot at the end of Pesach;
You swept and destroyed Egypt when passing on Pesach;
And you shall say: It is the Pesach sacrifice.

Lord, every Egyptian firstborn You did crush on Pesach;
But Your firstborn You did pass over on the Pesach;

120

לְבִלְתִּי תֵת מַשְׁחִית לָבֹא בִּפְתָחַי בַּפֶּסַח,
וַאֲמַרְתֶּם זֶבַח פֶּסַח.

מְסֻגֶּרֶת סֻגְּרָה בְּעִתּוֹתֵי פֶּסַח,
נִשְׁמְדָה מִדְיָן בִּצְלִיל שְׂעוֹרֵי עֹמֶר פֶּסַח,
שֹׂרְפוּ מִשְׁמַנֵּי פּוּל וְלוּד בִּיקַד יְקוֹד פֶּסַח,
וַאֲמַרְתֶּם זֶבַח פֶּסַח.

עוֹד הַיּוֹם בְּנֹב לַעֲמוֹד, עַד גָּעָה עוֹנַת פֶּסַח,
פַּס יָד כָּתְבָה לְקַעֲקֵעַ צוּל בַּפֶּסַח,
צָפֹה הַצָּפִית עָרוֹךְ הַשֻּׁלְחָן, בַּפֶּסַח,
וַאֲמַרְתֶּם זֶבַח פֶּסַח.

קָהָל כִּנְּסָה הֲדַסָּה צוֹם לְשַׁלֵּשׁ בַּפֶּסַח,
רֹאשׁ מִבֵּית רָשָׁע מָחַצְתָּ בְּעֵץ חֲמִשִּׁים בַּפֶּסַח,
שְׁתֵּי אֵלֶּה רֶגַע, תָּבִיא לְעוּצִית בַּפֶּסַח,
תָּעֹז יָדְךָ וְתָרוּם יְמִינְךָ, כְּלֵיל הִתְקַדֶּשׁ חַג פֶּסַח,
וַאֲמַרְתֶּם זֶבַח פֶּסַח.

So that no evil destroyed Israel's homes on Pesach;
And you shall say: It is the Pesach sacrifice.

The well-locked city of Jericho fell on Pesach;
Midian was destroyed through a barley-cake from the Omer of Pesach;
Assyria's mighty armies were consumed by fire on Pesach;
And you shall say: It is the Pesach sacrifice.

Sanncherib would have held his ground at Nov but for the siege on Pesach;
A hand inscribed Babylon's fate on Pesach;
Babylon's festive table was destroyed on Pesach;
And you shall say: It is the Pesach sacrifice.

Esther called a three-day feast on Pesach;
You did hang the evil Haman on Pesach;
Doubly, will You punish Edom on Pesach;
Let Your mighty arm save us from harm on the night of Pesach;
And you shall say: It is the Pesach sacrifice.

כִּי לוֹ נָאֶה, כִּי לוֹ יָאֶה

אַדִּיר בִּמְלוּכָה, בָּחוּר כַּהֲלָכָה, גְּדוּדָיו יֹאמְרוּ לוֹ:
לְךָ וּלְךָ, לְךָ כִּי לְךָ, לְךָ אַף לְךָ, לְךָ יהוה הַמַּמְלָכָה.
כִּי לוֹ נָאֶה, כִּי לוֹ יָאֶה.

דָּגוּל בִּמְלוּכָה, הָדוּר כַּהֲלָכָה, וָתִיקָיו יֹאמְרוּ לוֹ:
לְךָ וּלְךָ, לְךָ כִּי לְךָ, לְךָ אַף לְךָ, לְךָ יהוה הַמַּמְלָכָה.
כִּי לוֹ נָאֶה, כִּי לוֹ יָאֶה.

זַכַּאי בִּמְלוּכָה, חָסִין כַּהֲלָכָה, טַפְסְרָיו יֹאמְרוּ לוֹ:
לְךָ וּלְךָ, לְךָ כִּי לְךָ, לְךָ אַף לְךָ, לְךָ יהוה הַמַּמְלָכָה.
כִּי לוֹ נָאֶה, כִּי לוֹ יָאֶה.

יָחִיד בִּמְלוּכָה, כַּבִּיר כַּהֲלָכָה, לִמּוּדָיו יֹאמְרוּ לוֹ:
לְךָ וּלְךָ, לְךָ כִּי לְךָ, לְךָ אַף לְךָ, לְךָ יהוה הַמַּמְלָכָה.
כִּי לוֹ נָאֶה, כִּי לוֹ יָאֶה.

KI LO NAEH, KI LO YAEH

Powerful in kingship, truly chosen, His troops sing to Him:
To You and to You; To You and for You; To You, just for You; To You, O Lord,
is the sovereignty;
To Him praise is comely; To Him praise is becoming.

Famous in kingship, truly glorious, His faithful sing to Him:
To You and to You; To You and for You; To You, just for You; To You, O Lord,
is the sovereignty;
To Him praise is comely; To Him praise is becoming.

Guiltless in kingship, truly strong, His angels sing to Him:
To You and to You; To You and for You; To You, just for You; To You, O Lord,
is the sovereignty;
To Him praise is comely; To Him praise is becoming.
Alone in kingship, truly powerful, His scholars sing to Him:
To You and to You; To You and for You; To You, just for You; To You, O Lord,
is the sovereignty;
To Him praise is comely; To Him praise is becoming.

מוֹשֵׁל בִּמְלוּכָה, נוֹרָא כַּהֲלָכָה, סְבִיבָיו יֹאמְרוּ לוֹ:
לְךָ וּלְךָ, לְךָ כִּי לְךָ, לְךָ אַף לְךָ, לְךָ יהוה הַמַּמְלָכָה.
כִּי לוֹ נָאֶה, כִּי לוֹ יָאֶה.

עָנָו בִּמְלוּכָה, פּוֹדֶה כַּהֲלָכָה, צַדִּיקָיו יֹאמְרוּ לוֹ:
לְךָ וּלְךָ, לְךָ כִּי לְךָ, לְךָ אַף לְךָ, לְךָ יהוה הַמַּמְלָכָה.
כִּי לוֹ נָאֶה, כִּי לוֹ יָאֶה.

קָדוֹשׁ בִּמְלוּכָה, רַחוּם כַּהֲלָכָה, שִׁנְאַנָּיו יֹאמְרוּ לוֹ:
לְךָ וּלְךָ, לְךָ כִּי לְךָ, לְךָ אַף לְךָ, לְךָ יהוה הַמַּמְלָכָה.
כִּי לוֹ נָאֶה, כִּי לוֹ יָאֶה.

תַּקִּיף בִּמְלוּכָה, תּוֹמֵךְ כַּהֲלָכָה, תְּמִימָיו יֹאמְרוּ לוֹ:
לְךָ וּלְךָ, לְךָ כִּי לְךָ, לְךָ אַף לְךָ, לְךָ יהוה הַמַּמְלָכָה.
כִּי לוֹ נָאֶה, כִּי לוֹ יָאֶה.

Commanding in kingship, truly revered, His near ones sing to Him:
To You and to You; To You and for You; To You, just for You; To You, O Lord, is the sovereignty;
To Him praise is comely; To Him praise is becoming.

Humble in kingship, truly redeeming, His righteous sing to Him:
To You and to You; To You and for You; To You, just for You; To You, O Lord, is the sovereignty;
To Him praise is comely; To Him praise is becoming.

Holy in kingship, truly merciful, His angels sing to Him:
To You and to You; To You and for You; To You, just for You; To You, O Lord, is the sovereignty;
To Him praise is comely; To Him praise is becoming.

Indomitable in kingship, truly sustaining, His innocent sing to Him:
To You and to You; To You and for You; To You, just for You; To You, O Lord, is the sovereignty;
To Him praise is comely; To Him praise is becoming.

אַדִּיר הוּא, יִבְנֶה בֵיתוֹ בְּקָרוֹב, בִּמְהֵרָה בִּמְהֵרָה, בְּיָמֵינוּ בְּקָרוֹב. אֵל בְּנֵה, אֵל בְּנֵה, בְּנֵה בֵיתְךָ בְּקָרוֹב.

בָּחוּר הוּא, גָּדוֹל הוּא, דָּגוּל הוּא, יִבְנֶה בֵיתוֹ בְּקָרוֹב, בִּמְהֵרָה בִּמְהֵרָה, בְּיָמֵינוּ בְּקָרוֹב. אֵל בְּנֵה, אֵל בְּנֵה, בְּנֵה בֵיתְךָ בְּקָרוֹב.

הָדוּר הוּא, וָתִיק הוּא, זַכַּאי הוּא, חָסִיד הוּא, יִבְנֶה בֵיתוֹ בְּקָרוֹב, בִּמְהֵרָה בִּמְהֵרָה, בְּיָמֵינוּ בְּקָרוֹב. אֵל בְּנֵה, אֵל בְּנֵה, בְּנֵה בֵיתְךָ בְּקָרוֹב.

טָהוֹר הוּא, יָחִיד הוּא, כַּבִּיר הוּא, לָמוּד הוּא, מֶלֶךְ הוּא, נוֹרָא הוּא, סַגִּיב הוּא, עִזּוּז הוּא, פּוֹדֶה הוּא, צַדִּיק הוּא, יִבְנֶה בֵיתוֹ בְּקָרוֹב, בִּמְהֵרָה בִּמְהֵרָה, בְּיָמֵינוּ בְּקָרוֹב. אֵל בְּנֵה, אֵל בְּנֵה, בְּנֵה בֵיתְךָ בְּקָרוֹב.

קָדוֹשׁ הוּא, רַחוּם הוּא, שַׁדַּי הוּא, תַּקִּיף הוּא, יִבְנֶה בֵיתוֹ בְּקָרוֹב, בִּמְהֵרָה בִּמְהֵרָה, בְּיָמֵינוּ בְּקָרוֹב. אֵל בְּנֵה, אֵל בְּנֵה, בְּנֵה בֵיתְךָ בְּקָרוֹב.

ADIR HU

He is powerful, May He build His temple very soon. Speedily, speedily, in our days, very soon, O God build, O God build, build Your temple speedily.

He is chosen, great, famous; May He build His temple very soon. Speedily, speedily, in our days very soon, O God build, O God build, build Your temple speedily.

He is glorious, pure, guiltless, pious; May He build His temple very soon. Speedily, speedily, in our days very soon, O God build, O God build, build Your temple speedily.

He is clean, unique, powerful, learned, majestic, revered, eminent, strong, redeeming, righteous. May He build His temple very soon. Speedily, speedily, in our days very soon, O God build, O God build, build Your temple speedily.

He is holy, merciful, almighty, indomitable; May He build His temple very soon. Speedily, speedily, in our days very soon, O God build, O God build, build Your temple speedily.

ECHAD ME YODEA
WHO KNOWS ONE?

The Seder begins with questions – four to be exact – and ends with questions – thirteen to be exact. Beginning with "Who knows one?" we proceed one by one until we ask, "Who knows thirteen?" In some ways it is safe to say that only a Jew could have written this popular song. Hardly anyone else would write a song culminating with the number 13, widely considered to be unlucky.

Our society refers to the number 13 as being the "devil's dozen." There is a book, *Thirteen – The World's Most Popular Superstition* by Nathaniel Lachenmeyer. The fear of 13 even has an official name: Triskaidekaphobia. The popular belief that 13 is an unlucky number is derived from Christianity where Jesus' Last Supper was attended by him and his 12 disciples.

Whether 13 as "unlucky" is a Christian concept or not is open to question. There is no question that we Jews are "triskaidekaphiliacs" – those who think of 13 as a lucky number. A young man enters the adult congregation of Israel at the age of 13. Maimonides listed "13 Principles of Faith" that every Jew must believe. The numerical values of the Hebrew words for love (*ahavah*) and for one (*echad*) are both 13. Indeed, God is described as possessing "13 attributes."

This is but one of countless examples of how Jews look at the world differently. And while some resent us for that, the reality is that it has been our greatest strength. In one of his letters written in 1926, Sigmund Freud writes, "Because I was a Jew I found myself free from many prejudices which limited others in their employment of their intellects. And as a Jew I was prepared to go into opposition and do without the agreement of the compact majority."

By looking at things differently, by always questioning the accepted norms of society, the Jewish people have made lasting contributions to society. Perhaps this is best reflected in the following comparison of a list of the winners of the Nobel Prize from among the Muslim people and the Jewish people. Among the Muslims, there have been nine Nobel Prize winners: in Literature: Albert Camus and Najib Mahfooz. In Peace: Mohamed Anwar El-Sadat, Yasser Arafat and Mohamed Elbardel. In Chemistry: Elias James Corey and Ahmed Zewail. And in Medicine: Peter Brian Medawar and Ferid Mourad. That's nine Nobel Prize winners from a population of *1.2 billion* Muslims. Now, here are the names of the Jewish Nobel Prize winners:

Albert Abraham Michelson
Gabriel Lippmann
Albert Einstein
Niels Bohr
James Franck
Gustav Hertz
Otto Stern
Isidor Issac Rabi
Wolfgang Pauli
Felix Bloch
Max Born
Igor Tamm
Ll'ja Frank
Emilio Segre
Donald A. Glaser
Robert Hofstadter
Lev Davidovich Landau
Eugene Wigner
Richard Phillips Feynman
Julian Schwinger
Hans Bethe
Murray Gell-Mann
Dennis Gabor
Leon Cooper
Brian David Josephson
Benjamin Mottleson
Burton Richter

Arno Allan Penzias
Jack Steinberger
Peter L. Kapitza
Stephen Weinberg
Sheldon Glashow
Leon Lederman
Melvin Schwartz
Jack Steinberger
Jerome Friedman
Georges Charpak
Frederick Reines
Martin Perl
David Lee
Claude Cohen-Tannoudji
Zhores Alferov
Vataly Ginzburg
Alexi Abrikosov
David Politzer
David Gross
Roy Glauber

These are the Jewish Nobel Prize winners ... IN PHYSICS! Just in Physics there have been 47 Jewish Nobel Prize winners. Overall there have been more than 150! 9 from 1.2 billion Muslims. 150+ from 14 million Jews.

- Does that mean that Jews are smarter?
- That Jews are better?
- That Jews are different?
- That Jews see things differently?
- Do you?

אֶחָד מִי יוֹדֵעַ?

אֶחָד מִי יוֹדֵעַ?
אֶחָד אֲנִי יוֹדֵעַ: אֶחָד אֱלֹהֵינוּ שֶׁבַּשָּׁמַיִם וּבָאָרֶץ.

שְׁנַיִם מִי יוֹדֵעַ?
שְׁנַיִם אֲנִי יוֹדֵעַ: שְׁנֵי לֻחוֹת הַבְּרִית, אֶחָד אֱלֹהֵינוּ שֶׁבַּשָּׁמַיִם וּבָאָרֶץ.

שְׁלֹשָׁה מִי יוֹדֵעַ?
שְׁלֹשָׁה אֲנִי יוֹדֵעַ: שְׁלֹשָׁה אָבוֹת, שְׁנֵי לֻחוֹת הַבְּרִית, אֶחָד אֱלֹהֵינוּ שֶׁבַּשָּׁמַיִם וּבָאָרֶץ.

אַרְבַּע מִי יוֹדֵעַ?
אַרְבַּע אֲנִי יוֹדֵעַ: אַרְבַּע אִמָּהוֹת, שְׁלֹשָׁה אָבוֹת, שְׁנֵי לֻחוֹת הַבְּרִית, אֶחָד אֱלֹהֵינוּ שֶׁבַּשָּׁמַיִם וּבָאָרֶץ.

ECHAD MI YODEA?

Who knows one?
I know one! One is Hashem in the heavens and on the earth.

Who knows two?
I know two! Two are the tablets of the covenant; One is Hashem in the the heavens and on the earth.

Who knows three?
I know three! Three are the fathers (of Israel); Two are the tablets of the covenant; One is Hashem in the heavens and on the earth.

Who knows four?
I know four! Four are the mothers (of Israel); Three are the fathers (of Israel); Two are the tablets of the covenant; One is Hashem in the heavens and on the earth.

חֲמִשָּׁה מִי יוֹדֵעַ?
חֲמִשָּׁה אֲנִי יוֹדֵעַ: חֲמִשָּׁה חוּמְשֵׁי תוֹרָה, אַרְבַּע אִמָּהוֹת, שְׁלֹשָׁה אָבוֹת,
שְׁנֵי לֻחוֹת הַבְּרִית, אֶחָד אֱלֹהֵינוּ שֶׁבַּשָּׁמַיִם וּבָאָרֶץ.

שִׁשָּׁה מִי יוֹדֵעַ?
שִׁשָּׁה אֲנִי יוֹדֵעַ: שִׁשָּׁה סִדְרֵי מִשְׁנָה, חֲמִשָּׁה חוּמְשֵׁי תוֹרָה, אַרְבַּע
אִמָּהוֹת, שְׁלֹשָׁה אָבוֹת, שְׁנֵי לֻחוֹת הַבְּרִית, אֶחָד אֱלֹהֵינוּ שֶׁבַּשָּׁמַיִם וּבָאָרֶץ.

שִׁבְעָה מִי יוֹדֵעַ?
שִׁבְעָה אֲנִי יוֹדֵעַ: שִׁבְעָה יְמֵי שַׁבַּתָּא, שִׁשָּׁה סִדְרֵי מִשְׁנָה, חֲמִשָּׁה
חוּמְשֵׁי תוֹרָה, אַרְבַּע אִמָּהוֹת, שְׁלֹשָׁה אָבוֹת, שְׁנֵי לֻחוֹת הַבְּרִית,
אֶחָד אֱלֹהֵינוּ שֶׁבַּשָּׁמַיִם וּבָאָרֶץ.

שְׁמוֹנָה מִי יוֹדֵעַ?
שְׁמוֹנָה אֲנִי יוֹדֵעַ: שְׁמוֹנָה יְמֵי מִילָה, שִׁבְעָה יְמֵי שַׁבַּתָּא, שִׁשָּׁה
סִדְרֵי מִשְׁנָה, חֲמִשָּׁה חוּמְשֵׁי תוֹרָה, אַרְבַּע אִמָּהוֹת, שְׁלֹשָׁה
אָבוֹת, שְׁנֵי לֻחוֹת הַבְּרִית, אֶחָד אֱלֹהֵינוּ שֶׁבַּשָּׁמַיִם וּבָאָרֶץ.

Who knows five?
I know five! Five are the books of the Torah; Four are the mothers (of Israel); Three are the fathers (of Israel); Two are the tablets of the covenant; One is Hashem in the heavens and on the earth.

Who knows six?
I know six! Six are the orders of the Mishnah; Five are the books of the Torah; Four are the mothers (of Israel); Three are the fathers (of Israel); Two are the tablets of the covenant; One is Hashem in the heavens and on the earth.

Who knows seven?
I know seven! Seven are the days of the week; Six are the orders of the Mishnah; Five are the books of the Torah; Four are the mothers (of Israel); Three are the fathers (of Israel); Two are the tablets of the covenant; One is Hashem in the heavens and on the earth.

Who knows eight?
I know eight! Eight are the days to circumcision; Seven are the days of the week; Six are the orders of the Mishnah; Five are the books of the Torah; Four are the mothers (of Israel); Three are the fathers (of Israel); Two are the tablets of the covenant; One is Hashem in the heavens and on the earth.

תִּשְׁעָה מִי יוֹדֵעַ?

תִּשְׁעָה אֲנִי יוֹדֵעַ: תִּשְׁעָה יַרְחֵי לֵדָה, שְׁמוֹנָה יְמֵי מִילָה, שִׁבְעָה יְמֵי שַׁבַּתָּא, שִׁשָּׁה סִדְרֵי מִשְׁנָה, חֲמִשָּׁה חוּמְשֵׁי תוֹרָה, אַרְבַּע אִמָּהוֹת, שְׁלֹשָׁה אָבוֹת, שְׁנֵי לֻחוֹת הַבְּרִית, אֶחָד אֱלֹהֵינוּ שֶׁבַּשָּׁמַיִם וּבָאָרֶץ.

עֲשָׂרָה מִי יוֹדֵעַ?

עֲשָׂרָה אֲנִי יוֹדֵעַ: עֲשָׂרָה דִבְּרַיָּא, תִּשְׁעָה יַרְחֵי לֵדָה, שְׁמוֹנָה יְמֵי מִילָה, שִׁבְעָה יְמֵי שַׁבַּתָּא, שִׁשָּׁה סִדְרֵי מִשְׁנָה, חֲמִשָּׁה חוּמְשֵׁי תוֹרָה, אַרְבַּע אִמָּהוֹת, שְׁלֹשָׁה אָבוֹת, שְׁנֵי לֻחוֹת הַבְּרִית, אֶחָד אֱלֹהֵינוּ שֶׁבַּשָּׁמַיִם וּבָאָרֶץ.

אַחַד עָשָׂר מִי יוֹדֵעַ?

אַחַד עָשָׂר אֲנִי יוֹדֵעַ: אַחַד עָשָׂר כּוֹכְבַיָּא, עֲשָׂרָה דִבְּרַיָּא, תִּשְׁעָה יַרְחֵי לֵדָה, שְׁמוֹנָה יְמֵי מִילָה, שִׁבְעָה יְמֵי שַׁבַּתָּא, שִׁשָּׁה סִדְרֵי מִשְׁנָה, חֲמִשָּׁה חוּמְשֵׁי תוֹרָה, אַרְבַּע אִמָּהוֹת, שְׁלֹשָׁה אָבוֹת, שְׁנֵי לֻחוֹת הַבְּרִית, אֶחָד אֱלֹהֵינוּ שֶׁבַּשָּׁמַיִם וּבָאָרֶץ.

Who knows nine?
I know nine! Nine are the months to childbirth; Eight are the days to circumcision; Seven are the days of the week; Six are the orders of the Mishnah; Five are the books of the Torah; Four are the mothers (of Israel); Three are the fathers (of Israel); Two are the tablets of the covenant; One is Hashem in the heavens and on the earth.

Who knows ten?
I know ten! Ten are the commandments; Nine are the months to childbirth; Eight are the days to circumcision; Seven are the days of the week; Six are the orders of the Mishnah; Five are the books of the Torah; Four are the mothers (of Israel); Three are the fathers (of Israel); Two are the tablets of the covenant; One is Hashem in the heavens and on the earth.

Who knows eleven?
I know eleven! Eleven are the stars (in Joseph's dream); Ten are the commandments; Nine are the months to childbirth; Eight are the days to circumcision; Seven are the days of the week; Six are the orders of the Mishnah; Five are the books of the Torah; Four are the mothers (of Israel); Three are the fathers (of Israel); Two are the tablets of the covenant; One is Hashem in the heavens and on the earth.

שְׁנֵים עָשָׂר מִי יוֹדֵעַ?
שְׁנֵים עָשָׂר אֲנִי יוֹדֵעַ: שְׁנֵים עָשָׂר שִׁבְטַיָּא, אַחַד עָשָׂר כּוֹכְבַיָּא, עֲשָׂרָה דִבְּרַיָּא, תִּשְׁעָה יַרְחֵי לֵדָה, שְׁמוֹנָה יְמֵי מִילָה, שִׁבְעָה יְמֵי שַׁבַּתָּא, שִׁשָּׁה סִדְרֵי מִשְׁנָה, חֲמִשָּׁה חוּמְשֵׁי תוֹרָה, אַרְבַּע אִמָּהוֹת, שְׁלֹשָׁה אָבוֹת, שְׁנֵי לֻחוֹת הַבְּרִית, אֶחָד אֱלֹהֵינוּ שֶׁבַּשָּׁמַיִם וּבָאָרֶץ.

שְׁלֹשָׁה עָשָׂר מִי יוֹדֵעַ?
שְׁלֹשָׁה עָשָׂר אֲנִי יוֹדֵעַ: שְׁלֹשָׁה עָשָׂר מִדַּיָּא, שְׁנֵים עָשָׂר שִׁבְטַיָּא, אַחַד עָשָׂר כּוֹכְבַיָּא, עֲשָׂרָה דִבְּרַיָּא, תִּשְׁעָה יַרְחֵי לֵדָה, שְׁמוֹנָה יְמֵי מִילָה, שִׁבְעָה יְמֵי שַׁבַּתָּא, שִׁשָּׁה סִדְרֵי מִשְׁנָה, חֲמִשָּׁה חוּמְשֵׁי תוֹרָה, אַרְבַּע אִמָּהוֹת, שְׁלֹשָׁה אָבוֹת, שְׁנֵי לֻחוֹת הַבְּרִית, אֶחָד אֱלֹהֵינוּ שֶׁבַּשָּׁמַיִם וּבָאָרֶץ.

Who knows twelve?
I know twelve! Twelve are the tribes (of Israel); Eleven are the stars (in Joseph's dream); Ten are the commandments; Nine are the months to childbirth; Eight are the days to circumcision; Seven are the days of the week; Six are the orders of the Mishnah; Five are the books of the Torah; Four are the mothers (of Israel); Three are the fathers (of Israel); Two are the tablets of the covenant; One is Hashem in the heavens and on the earth.

Who knows thirteen?
I know thirteen! Thirteen are the attributes of God; Twelve are the tribes (of Israel); Eleven are the stars (in Joseph's dream); Ten are the commandments; Nine are the months to childbirth; Eight are the days to circumcision; Seven are the days of the week; Six are the orders of the Mishnah; Five are the books of the Torah; Four are the mothers (of Israel); Three are the fathers (of Israel); Two are the tablets of the covenant; One is Hashem in the heavens and on the earth.

CHAD GADYA
ONE KID

Written in Aramaic, the song "Chad Gadya," despite being sung at a late hour, always captures the imagination of children and adults alike. But is it possible that the Pesach Seder ends with a song that has been compared to such nursery rhymes as "The House that Jack Built?" Is there not a deeper meaning to this song? There certainly is! As stated in the Silverman Haggadah, Rabbi Jonathan Eybeschutz, a famed 18th century scholar, has interpreted "Chad Gadya" as a hymn to God's providence. God is evident in the history of humanity. Israel (The Kid), redeemed by God from Egypt through Moses and Aaron (the two Zuzim), succumbs to a mightier empire which, in turn, is defeated by other empires, until God's rule of justice triumphs. The cat is Assyria; the dog, Babylonia; the stick, Persia; the water, Greece; the ox, Rome; the slaughterer, the Muslims; the angel of death, the European nations. The Holy One will finally suppress all tyranny, deliver all His children from oppression, re-establish the principle of justice, and bring about the era of peace for all nations.

This is a beautiful explanation, bringing great meaning to a seemingly simple song. There is only one problem: the explanation makes no sense. If the Chad Gadya – the one child – is meant to represent the Jewish people, then we should have disappeared a long time ago! At the beginning of the song we are told that the "one kid" was slain by the cat, who in turn was slain by others. We Jews were supposed to disappear from the world scene thousands of years ago. And yet, we haven't. It makes no sense. How was it possible?

There is only one explanation: it's a miracle … the miracle of Jewish survival, the redemption of God's promise to Abraham made thousands of years ago that His people would be made into a "mighty nation." We are the generation of our people that has seen this promise fulfilled. And as one looks at the empires that dreamed of Jewish destruction – an

Egypt, a Babylon, a Greece, a Rome, a Spain – all glories of generations past, surely the power of that heavenly promise must be felt.

The little "kid" is alive and well and still kicking!

• Are you proud of being Jewish?
• What are you doing to help perpetuate the Jewish people?

חַד גַּדְיָא, חַד גַּדְיָא. דְּזַבִּין (דְּזְבַן) אַבָּא בִּתְרֵי זוּזֵי, חַד גַּדְיָא, חַד גַּדְיָא.

וְאָתָא שׁוּנְרָא, וְאָכְלָה לְגַדְיָא, דְּזַבִּין (דְּזְבַן) אַבָּא בִּתְרֵי זוּזֵי, חַד גַּדְיָא,
חַד גַּדְיָא.

וְאָתָא כַלְבָּא, וְנָשַׁךְ לְשׁוּנְרָא, דְּאָכְלָה לְגַדְיָא, דְּזַבִּין (דְּזְבַן) אַבָּא בִּתְרֵי
זוּזֵי, חַד גַּדְיָא, חַד גַּדְיָא.

וְאָתָא חוּטְרָא, וְהִכָּה לְכַלְבָּא, דְּנָשַׁךְ לְשׁוּנְרָא, דְּאָכְלָה לְגַדְיָא,דְּזַבִּין
(דְּזְבַן) אַבָּא בִּתְרֵי זוּזֵי, חַד גַּדְיָא, חַד גַּדְיָא.

וְאָתָא נוּרָא, וְשָׂרַף לְחוּטְרָא, דְּהִכָּה לְכַלְבָּא, דְּנָשַׁךְ לְשׁוּנְרָא, דְּאָכְלָה
לְגַדְיָא, דְּזַבִּין (דְּזְבַן) אַבָּא בִּתְרֵי זוּזֵי, חַד גַּדְיָא, חַד גַּדְיָא.

וְאָתָא מַיָּא, וְכָבָה לְנוּרָא, דְּשָׂרַף לְחוּטְרָא, דְּהִכָּה לְכַלְבָּא, דְּנָשַׁךְ לְשׁוּנְרָא,
דְּאָכְלָה לְגַדְיָא, דְּזַבִּין (דְּזְבַן) אַבָּא בִּתְרֵי זוּזֵי, חַד גַּדְיָא, חַד גַּדְיָא.

CHAD GADYAH

One kid, one kid that father bought for two zuzim; One kid, one kid.

The cat came and ate the kid that father bought for two zuzim; One kid, one kid.

The dog came and bit the cat that ate the kid that father bought for two zuzim; One kid, one kid.

The stick came and beat the dog that bit the cat that ate the kid that father bought for two zuzim; One kid, one kid.

The fire came and burned the stick that beat the dog that bit the cat that ate the kid that father bought for two zuzim; One kid, one kid.

The water came and quenched the fire that burned the stick that beat the dog that bit the cat that ate the kid that father bought for two zuzim; One kid, one kid.

וְאָתָא תוֹרָא, וְשָׁתָא לְמַיָּא, דְּכָבָה לְנוּרָא, דְּשָׂרַף לְחוּטְרָא, דְּהִכָּה לְכַלְבָּא, דְּנָשַׁךְ לְשׁוּנְרָא, דְּאָכְלָה לְגַדְיָא, דְּזַבִּין (דְּזְבַן) אַבָּא בִּתְרֵי זוּזֵי, חַד גַּדְיָא, חַד גַּדְיָא.

וְאָתָא הַשּׁוֹחֵט, וְשָׁחַט לְתוֹרָא, דְּשָׁתָא לְמַיָּא, דְּכָבָה לְנוּרָא, דְּשָׂרַף לְחוּטְרָא, דְּהִכָּה לְכַלְבָּא, דְּנָשַׁךְ לְשׁוּנְרָא, דְּאָכְלָה לְגַדְיָא, דְּזַבִּין (דְּזְבַן) אַבָּא בִּתְרֵי זוּזֵי, חַד גַּדְיָא, חַד גַּדְיָא.

וְאָתָא מַלְאַךְ הַמָּוֶת, וְשָׁחַט לְשׁוֹחֵט, דְּשָׁחַט לְתוֹרָא, דְּשָׁתָא לְמַיָּא, דְּכָבָה לְנוּרָא, דְּשָׂרַף לְחוּטְרָא, דְּהִכָּה לְכַלְבָּא, דְּנָשַׁךְ לְשׁוּנְרָא, דְּאָכְלָה לְגַדְיָא, דְּזַבִּין (דְּזְבַן) אַבָּא בִּתְרֵי זוּזֵי, חַד גַּדְיָא, חַד גַּדְיָא.

וְאָתָא הַקָּדוֹשׁ בָּרוּךְ הוּא, וְשָׁחַט לְמַלְאַךְ הַמָּוֶת, דְּשָׁחַט לְשׁוֹחֵט, דְּשָׁחַט לְתוֹרָא, דְּשָׁתָא לְמַיָּא, דְּכָבָה לְנוּרָא, דְּשָׂרַף לְחוּטְרָא, דְּהִכָּה לְכַלְבָּא, דְּנָשַׁךְ לְשׁוּנְרָא, דְּאָכְלָה לְגַדְיָא, דְּזַבִּין (דְּזְבַן) אַבָּא בִּתְרֵי זוּזֵי, חַד גַּדְיָא, חַד גַּדְיָא.

The ox came and drank the water that quenched the fire that burned the stick that beat the dog that bit the cat that ate the kid that father bought for two zuzim; One kid, one kid.

The slaughterer came and killed the ox that drank the water that quenched the fire that burned the stick that beat the dog that bit the cat that ate the kid that father bought for two zuzim; One kid, one kid.

The angel of death came and slew the slaughterer that killed the ox that drank the water that quenched the fire that burned the stick that beat the dog that bit the cat that ate the kid that father bought for two zuzim; One kid, one kid.

The Holy One, blessed be He, came and slew the angel of death that slew the slaughterer that killed the ox that drank the water that quenched the fire that burned the stick that beat the dog that bit the cat that ate the kid that father bought for two zuzim; One kid, one kid.

10 Plagues – 10 Commandments
10 Questions for the Pesach Seder

1. Does sitting at a Seder in a hotel provide the same nostalgic memories as a Seder at home? What are your memories of Seders past?

2. What if "Bitter Herb" is your brother-in-law? How should he be treated at the Seder? What if he isn't Jewish?

3. In Israel a survey was taken to determine who is the greatest Jew who ever lived. Who would you choose? Would you want him/her at your Seder? If not, then who?

4. Would you consider someone like Jesus or Karl Marx a great Jew? What makes one a Jew?

5. In the Kiddush we speak of God as having "chosen us from all the nations." Did He/She? And if so, why? For what? For us to be blamed for everything including tsunamis?

6. In the Haggadah the name of Moses is mentioned only once in passing so as to focus on God as being the one who took the Jews out of Egypt. Do you believe in a God who is directly involved in our lives?

7. What do Pesach and Easter have in common? Spring festivals? Eggs? Redemption? How do they differ?

8. Who does the "wicked" child refer to? Saddam Hussein? Osama bin Laden? Mel Gibson? Your mother-in-law? What makes someone "wicked?"

9. Does freedom bring with it rights or responsibilities? What's the difference between the two?

10. Will your great-grandchildren be sitting at a Pesach Seder?

RABBI MITCHELL WOHLBERG

Since February 1, 1978, Mitchell S. Wohlberg has been the rabbi of the Beth Tfiloh Congregation, the largest Modern Orthodox synagogue in the United States. The year 2003 marked his 25th anniversary as the synagogue's spiritual leader. Through its various affiliates and its own day school of over 1000 students, Beth Tfiloh services 3,000 families. Rabbi Wohlberg is also the Dean of the Beth Tfiloh Community School, including the high school he helped establish in 1986. Described as the "Master of the Sermon" by The Baltimore Jewish Times, his sermons reach thousands both nationally and internationally by way of the Internet. His sermons can be read on the Beth Tfiloh website: www.BethTfiloh.com.

Rabbi Wohlberg was born in Brooklyn, NY on November 1, 1944. He received the Bachelor of Arts degree, Master of Hebrew Literature degree and rabbinic ordination from Yeshiva University. Upon receiving his rabbinic ordination, Rabbi Wohlberg, his father and his brothers were honored by Yeshiva University for being the first family in which three brothers and their father all received rabbinic ordination from that institution.

During his years of service to the Jewish community, Rabbi Wohlberg has been the recipient of the Humanitarian Award from the Louis Z. Brandeis District of the Zionist Organization of America, the Fellowship Award from Bar-Ilan University, the Lifetime Achievement Award from the Shaarei Zedek Medical Center in Jerusalem, and a scholarship has been established in his honor at Yeshiva University. He is also the recipient of the Golden Shofar Award from the State of Israel Bonds, and has been honored by the Crohn's & Colitis Foundation of America. In November 1998, Rabbi Wohlberg was presented with the "Rabbinical Award" by the UJA Federations of North America at the General Assembly held in Jerusalem. He presently serves on the International Board of Governors of Bar Ilan University.

Since 1966 he has been married to Sherry Kwestel Wohlberg, who received her Master of Social Work degree from Catholic University. The Wohlbergs are the proud parents of two sons, Andrew and Jonathan, and their daughters-in-law, Elizabeth and Melissa, as well as the joyous grandparents of Ella Chaya and Emuna Lev.

Made in the USA
Middletown, DE
04 April 2019